I0093374

INERTIA

INERTIA

Purposeful Inefficiencies in Financial Markets

YUVAL MILLO, CRAWFORD SPENCE, AND JAMES J. VALENTINE

Columbia University Press

New York

Columbia University Press
Publishers Since 1893
New York   Chichester, West Sussex

Copyright © 2025 Columbia University Press
All rights reserved

Library of Congress Cataloging-in-Publication Data
Names: Millo, Yuval, 1969– author. | Spence, Crawford, author.
| Valentine, James J, author.
Title: Inertia : purposeful inefficiencies in financial markets /
Yuval Millo, Crawford Spence, and James J. Valentine.
Description: New York : Columbia University Press, [2025] |
Includes index.
Identifiers: LCCN 2024031601 | ISBN 9780231212229
(hardback) | ISBN 9780231212236 (trade paperback) | ISBN
9780231559270 (ebook)
Subjects: LCSH: Investment advisors. | Investment analysis. |
Economics—Sociological aspects.
Classification: LCC HG4621 .M56 2025 | DDC 332.63/ 2042—
dc23/eng/20240823

Cover design: Noah Arlow
Cover image: Shutterstock

CONTENTS

Acknowledgments   *vii*

Introduction   1

1   Financial Intermediaries   13

2   Social Structures of Financial Markets   33

3   Social Stickiness   54

4   Conformity and Consensus   83

5   Technological Resistance   104

6   The Big Doxic Disturbance   134

7   Distinction Work   154

   Conclusion: Purposeful Inertia in
   Financial Markets   179

   *Methodological Appendix: Speaking to the
   Prophets of Alpha*   *195*

   Notes   *207*

   Index   *227*

ACKNOWLEDGMENTS

THIS BOOK is the culmination of a project that started back in 2018 and several people have helped us along the way, in different capacities. We have presented aspects of the work or the entire project at a variety of venues and so thank participants at seminars or conferences at: the University of Bristol; the London School of Economics and Political Science; Cardiff University; the Society for the Advancement of Socio-Economics annual conferences in Amsterdam in 2022 and Rio in 2023; the Behavioural Finance Working Group annual conference in London in 2023; the Finwork Futures research centre at King's College London; Copenhagen Business School; the University of York; the Centre for Professional Services Firms at City University, London; Concordia University; and DePaul University.

Certain key individuals have been important interlocutors as our ideas have developed over the course of the last few years, notably, Mark Aleksanyan, Chris Carter, Chris Chapman, Zhong Chen, Arman Eshraghi, Mahmoud Ezzamel, Adam Hayes, Ken Lee,

Andrea Mennicken, John Millar, Robin Powell, Alex Preda, Rita Samiolo, Len Seabrooke, Richard Taffler, Ane Tamayo, Hendrik Vollmer, and Mingzhu Wang. Special thanks go from Yuval Millo to Donald MacKenzie for his ongoing mentorship and to Mike Power for offering a first chance in academia. James Valentine would like to acknowledge those who led him to pursue projects such as the one that led to this book, specifically, Erich Dierdorff, Grace Lemmon, Albert Muñiz, Richard Rocco and Robert Rubin.

The team at Columbia University Press has been excellent throughout, notably Eric Schwartz, Alyssa Napier, and Marielle Poss. The editor Eric Schwartz championed the project from the beginning. He provided invaluable advice on how to frame our arguments during various drafts and also how to respond to the detailed comments of two anonymous reviewers who were enlisted to comment on both the book proposal and the first full draft. We acknowledge the constructive impact of those two reviewers here as well.

We also thank the seventy financial intermediaries who agreed to be interviewed. The project would not have been possible had these individuals not graciously provided their time and reflections for us to mull over, dissect and critique.

Projects of this scope and length become relatively fixed features of personal lives for their duration, as family members are all too aware. Crawford Spence would like to acknowledge the loving support of Lucie, Nikita, Fintan, Estelle, Freddie, and Monty. Yuval Millo would like to acknowledge the support of Hadas, Noa, and Michael. You guys are the best. James Valentine would like to acknowledge the support of his family Emma, Laura, Robert, and Alice.

INERTIA

INTRODUCTION

PREAMBLE

Conventional wisdom tells us that financial intermediaries are somehow essential to helping individuals and institutions navigate the increasingly complex world of modern-day financial markets. For example, Investopedia—a barometer of conventional financial wisdom if ever there was one—says this about the value that financial intermediaries bring: "Financial intermediaries help create efficient markets and lower the cost of doing business. . . . Financial intermediaries offer the benefit of pooling risk, reducing cost, and providing economies of scale, among others."[1] Apparently there are no downsides to financial intermediation, only benefits. This is fairly hyperbolic and devoid of reflexivity, even by Investopedia standards.

As John Kenneth Galbraith has astutely pointed out, conventional wisdom can act as a way to circumvent painful thinking.[2] Yet it doesn't take much digging around to find people who have undertaken the painful job of thinking about financial intermediaries—and, indeed, critical interpretations abound. For example, journalists regularly produce accounts of fund managers who manage to recoup large sums in fees even when their clients are losing money.[3] Economists have shown quite comprehensively in study after study how active fund managers routinely underperform low-cost index funds. One recent contribution to this canon provided a 30-year comparison of the performance of U.S. mutual funds with that of the exchange-traded fund (ETF) SPY, which offers a low-cost means of investing in the whole S&P 500. The results suggest an "aggregate wealth loss of $1.02 trillion to mutual fund investors" over the time period.[4] More-niche academic analyses on equity research tend to show how analysts in investment banks appear to offer very little value to their institutional clients,[5] while sociological framings illustrate how financial intermediation has progressively retained more and more economic capital for itself over the last 150 years despite growing economies of scale and technological innovation.[6] Whatever one's vantage point, there is much for which to take financial intermediaries to task.

However, what these accounts do not explain is how financial intermediaries successfully persist in financial markets despite such criticisms and concerns over their remuneration, impact, and value. This is what we explore in this book: specifically, we look at how various groups of financial intermediaries who make up the active investment community owe their livelihoods, at least in part, to congealed social relations and ossified ideas that are difficult to shift even though it would seem to be economically expedient to do so.

Not only does this give us a new way of explaining the dynamics surrounding financial intermediation, but also it paves the way to a new understanding of financial markets more broadly. According to conventional wisdom, financial markets are driven by innovation, dynamism, and continual disruption. It is all too often overlooked that financial markets are really just like any other field in social life, populated by humans who tend to hire people they like, engage in practices because they have always done so rather than because these make the most economic sense, and are subject to the reality of power relations that place constraints on their agency. Because of these and many other factors, financial markets have inertial tendencies. These tendencies need to be recognized and feature in our conceptualizations of both financial markets and the intermediaries who populate them.

WHAT WE EXPLORE IN THE BOOK

In this book, we examine the practices and interactions that surround investment decision-making by asset managers. Specifically we look at how the buy-side, which consists of fund managers, hedge fund managers, and in-house analysts, develops relationships with sell-side analysts from investment banks and with corporate managers that both grow and congeal over time. In chapter 1, we explain in descriptive terms how those who make up this cast of characters routinely interact with one another in financial markets. This explanation will be particularly helpful to those who are less well acquainted with those on the buy-side and sell-side and/or with how they tend to interact with one another on a routine basis in order to support investment decision-making.

Our intellectual framing in the book, which we present in chapter 2, draws primarily from the sociological work of Pierre Bourdieu and Marc Granovetter, two theorists who emphasize in different ways the social underpinnings of economic action. This framework leads to a view of the world of professional investing as a social field that is riven by a major schism between the active investment community (those who believe it is possible to beat the market) and the passive investment community (those who do not believe it is possible to beat the market). From the outset, it would appear that these two communities possess very different financial epistemologies, although how they react when their fundamental assumptions about how to invest are challenged is an empirical question.

With the rise of passive investing in the form of index funds and ETFs, the active investment community's legitimacy has come under scrutiny. Concomitantly so has the financial knowledge that underpins the wide panoply of active investing strategies identified in financial markets today. In order to adapt to the increasing fee pressure and investment outflows that many active funds have experienced in recent years as a result of the rise of passive investing,[7] we might suppose that different kinds of financial knowledge would be incubating in the laboratories of the active investment community. However, on the basis of the evidence we present in this book, this does not appear to be the case.

Communities that are under threat tend to become more vocal and explicit in how they talk about themselves.[8] This affords researchers an opportunity to gaze into both their epistemic assumptions and the social structures that underpin these, and this is exactly what we do here. Effectively, we look at the dense, congealed social networks that form over time among key actors in the active investment space. These congealed networks form the basis of an epistemic regime,[9] or knowledge base, that has interpersonal and interinstitutional support, both of which go a long way toward explaining why this epistemic regime persists despite internal and external challenges.

This results in a dense social network that provides stability to the field of investment advice. In chapter 3, we describe in detail this network and the social stickiness that binds it together. Moreover, we allude to the ways in which social stickiness often overrides meritocracy or utility when it comes to explaining why financial intermediaries interact with one another.

This social stickiness nevertheless is the source of rich interactions among buy-side, sell-side, and corporate actors. These interactions are characterized by face-to-face encounters, strong attention to narrative detail, and time spent together in order to add color to existing investment narratives, or challenge one another's views on the prospects of particular stocks or industry trends. This intellectual jousting, which is both the product and the basis of congealed relationships in the field of investment advice, stands in contrast to the ways that financial intermediaries (those on the sell-side, in particular) are perceived by the wider market, which is generally via very reductive calculations such as earnings forecasts and price targets that are used by the wider market to form consensus numbers. In other words, while the expertise of financial intermediaries is cultivated via dense networks and deep connections ("strong ties," to use Granovetter's language[10]), status and legitimacy are often conferred via a much shallower set of metrics.

This mismatch between the substantive work undertaken by intermediaries and the way they are perceived is common to many expert fields. Richard Sennett notes in *The Craftsman* that craftsmanship requires steady, focused, repetitive dedication to tasks in a relatively closed environment.[11] Yet recognition of craftsmanship is often the preserve of a wider community. For example, we witness this in our own field of academia, where scholars might pride themselves on offering relatively specific contributions to what might seem to be very niche areas. This book is no different. We undertake an economic sociology interpretation of how knowledge production by financial intermediaries is grounded in particular social structures, which sounds highly specialized. Yet our line managers might ask us more reductive questions such as "Who is publishing it?" or "How many citations will it yield?" rather than discussing the substantive content with us. Family doctors might pride themselves on understanding the detailed case histories of their patients and working closely with them to land on the correct diagnosis, but their supervisors might be more concerned with whether they exceeded their allotted twelve-minute appointment duration in doing so because this is what they are being measured on by wider regulatory authorities.

Similarly, financial intermediaries might see themselves as trusted investment consiglieri who have a lot to offer their buy-side clients by acting as a rich sounding board for ideas, yet they find themselves mostly scrutinized and judged on whether or not their earnings forecasts are accurate (although most fund managers claim not to have an interest in this). We explore these dynamics in chapter 4, where we describe the institutional pressures on sell-side analysts to conform to consensus numbers. For the purposes of the present book, this is interesting because it demonstrates how a dense social network acts to cultivate strong social ties and a relatively solid epistemic regime, yet it also encourages the flow of relatively shallow and weak information signals from that network to the wider market. Conceptually this shows how financial intermediaries are under contradictory pressures to be distinctive and to herd together at the same time, forcing them to play a dual game that challenges their identity.

The field of investment advice has its rules of the game, which are structured and written vis-à-vis these relationships among the field's actors. These rules become internalized and take the form of long-lasting dispositions of the mind and body, or *habitus*, as Bourdieu pithily summarizes the process of rule absorption.[12] The epistemic regime of the active fund management community is a key aspect of this active investor habitus.[13] In chapter 5, we elucidate key aspects of the active epistemic regime and habitus by exploring how financial intermediaries talk about the potentially disruptive role of technology. Field actors view technology with suspicion; they see is as something that might be an interesting investment object or societal trend but not something that can massively help their investment process. Instead, the unique selling points of the active investment community are small data and rich interpersonal interactions with knowledgeable actors from both within and outside the field. These actors embrace technology on certain levels, of course, but mostly where it helps with efficiently organizing work or tracking client interactions such that billing efficiency and accuracy are increased.

Having established the main epistemic contours of the active investing habitus, in chapters 6 and 7 we report on a direct challenge to this. The growth of passive investing strategies threatens the status and potentially the very existence of actively minded financial intermediaries. How they respond to this threat intellectually reveals the solidity of their epistemic regime. We find cognitive dissonance in this respect, with many actors conceding the superiority of passive funds to the point where some even admit to investing their own money in index vehicles. However, this seemingly defeatist stance is coupled with a robust intellectual defense. Active investing is seen as superior in many respects and, indeed, necessary to the health, vitality, and efficiency of the wider market. This epistemological chauvinism shows the solidity of the active community's epistemic regime and the extent to which social and mental structures are congealed in the field of investment advice.

We conclude the book with a synthesis of the various ideas and findings that we highlight in the previous substantive chapters. Specifically, we advance the idea of *purposeful inertia* to capture the complex reproduction of ideas and relationships in the field of investment advice. We stress that the inertia we identify is not a product of lethargy or laziness but rather is *purposeful* because a lot of energy goes into defending and maintaining the status quo.

For those interested in how we police our own epistemic regime, we describe our research methods and methodology in an appendix. It contains more detail about the people we spoke to, why we spoke to them, and how we analyzed the data, including explanations of coding techniques and data aggregation procedures. This is placed in an appendix so as not to disrupt the flow of the general argument.

CONCLUSION

In this book, we make a number of key conceptual arguments that advance our thinking about the social underpinnings of economic action in financial markets. First, we should not view financial intermediation as if it was immune to habits, routines, and social mores. The field of investment advice is a field like any other and includes all the interesting imperfections and idiosyncrasies that we would find in other fields of human action where people hire their friends, can't be bothered to change things that they know should probably be changed, and struggle to convince their superiors to do things a different way. We advance the concept of *purposeful inertia* to capture these various phenomena, as it speaks to the ways in which groups of actors work hard to maintain sticky relationships and ossified ideas in financial markets.

Second, the findings here call for a move beyond purely behavioral approaches to understanding economic behavior. Behavioral schools of thought have appeal far beyond academia these days, even as far as government policy units.[14] While any attempt to break free of the intellectual shackles of neoclassical economics is welcome, behavioral economics does not go far enough in our view. The decisions that people make are never merely cognitive or the product of a purely microlevel phenomenon. What we show in this book is that epistemic patterns and economic decisions always have a social basis, and, thus, it is not possible to explain economic action without also paying attention to the social structures that support it.

Third, we demonstrate how financial markets need to be understood not as overarching entities that tend only toward dynamism or innovation or conversely only toward stasis or inertia. Financial markets exhibit all of these tendencies, but much like capitalism itself, they are ultimately variegated, populated by heterogeneous communities or subfields whose habits, thinking, and relationships both congeal and evolve slowly, if at all.[15]

Fourth, we show how actors within fields have to play at least two games at once in order to maintain or improve their field position: they need to be both distinctive and conformist at the same time. Actors develop expertise and relevant knowledge on the basis of strong ties that have a biographical character to them. While these strong ties are important for career progression and status, recognition in a field often requires appeal to a broader community that does not have the bandwidth to appreciate the substantive expertise of actors. Strong networks therefore tend to send weak information signals as field members herd together. As such, whereas some studies have pointed toward the nature of herding[16] or boldness[17] in financial markets, our approach highlights these as epiphenomena that have a deeper basis in social structures. Moreover, the relatively super-ficial signals that dense networks emit also start to demonstrate the wider point that strong communities or clubs in financial markets don't necessarily produce strong or valuable outputs.

Finally, we offer new insights into how communities behave when they are under threat. Whereas previous research has found that threatened communities respond by asserting strong identities, framing practice areas as inaccessible to others, and delegitimizing competitors,[18] we show that, in addition, these communities engage in hopeful fantasizing. In some ways, this should not be a surprise, as self-delusion is a key feature of the human condition. However, it does take works such as the present one to remind us that these phenomena are just as prevalent in financial markets as they are in other walks of life. Whereas much thinking on financial intermediation looks at how infor-mation is transmitted from one expert party to another, often drawing an implicit contrast with the less informative noise that retail traders are purported to generate,[19] what we imply in this book is that everything in financial markets is noise. What is framed by groups of financial intermediaries as sophisticated knowledge may well have a seemingly strong epistemic basis and be supported by, for example, fundamental analysis, unique insights garnered from channel checks and expert networks, or privileged access to corporate insiders, but it is often recur-sive in nature. Moreover, as study after study has proved, these insights don't seem to generate alpha, excess return in compar-ison to a benchmark such as an index fund, over the long term. As a result, we conclude that the various communities that constitute financial markets are all responsible for conducting their own closed philosophical parlor games whose seeming erudition belies the fact that they are ultimately tantamount to noise. These parlor games also reflect a deeper truth: financial markets are socially constructed. They are made by humans in idiosyncratic ways. This implies that they can be unmade and reconstructed as well.

Chapter One

FINANCIAL INTERMEDIARIES

FINANCIAL INTERMEDIARIES AND THE INVESTMENT CHAIN

In this book, we explore the dynamics of financial intermediaries who work in the asset management industry. Specifically, we look at the two sets of practices and worldviews that are commonly designated as *sell-side* and *buy-side* in the professional investing world. Later we will elaborate on these labels and what they denote, but we start by zooming out and encapsulating what we understand to be *financial intermediation* in the context of asset management and professional investing. For this purpose, we draw initially on the work of Diane-Laure Arjaliès et al., who have elaborated the concept of the investment chain.[1]

Intermediation denotes the use of middlemen, and in the context of finance, this refers to a raft of investment advisers, lawyers, actuaries, consultants, fund managers, and analysts, among others, who are responsible for a large variety of practices related to handling *other* people's money. Emphasizing *other* is crucial here because commonsense understandings of groups that are widely perceived as professional investors don't capture the fundamental reality that these groups provide investment advice on and invest and execute trades with money that is generally not their own. They are entrusted with performing these various practices by others who are often quite unaware of how complex, multifaceted, and interconnected the field of investing is in reality.

Figure 1.1 captures in broad terms some of the complexity of financial intermediation in the context of investment management. On level 1 of the chain are investors (these could be individuals, companies that make investments from their own balance sheets, or governments that invest in partially nationalized utilities). They are generally removed by several levels of intermediation from the investment objects, those things in which they are ultimately investing at level 6. Between the investors and the investment objects are various investment vehicles at level 2, which are organizations, either permanent or ad hoc (these could be workplace pensions in which people are automatically enrolled, funds set up by financial advisers that individuals seek advice from, or even insurance policies, which make many of us inadvertent investors), that provide a managerial and organizational overlay to the funds and other vehicles that actually make investment decisions. These investment vehicles hire investment consultants to advise them on the mutual funds or hedge funds in which they might invest their clients' money. We can see that even before we reach level 3 of the investment chain, there are intermediaries that interact

Level 1: Investors

Level 2:
Asset Allocators

Level 3: Investment Management

Level 4: Investment Banks

Level 5: The Market

Level 6: Investment Objects

		Individuals, Companies, Charities, Governments		
Advisers and Wealth Managers	Sovereign Wealth Funds		Pension Funds	Insurance Companies
	Asset Managers and Buy-Side Analysts			
	Brokers, Sell-Side Analysts			
	Stock Exchanges, Over-the-Counter Venues, Dark Pools			
	Companies, Governments			

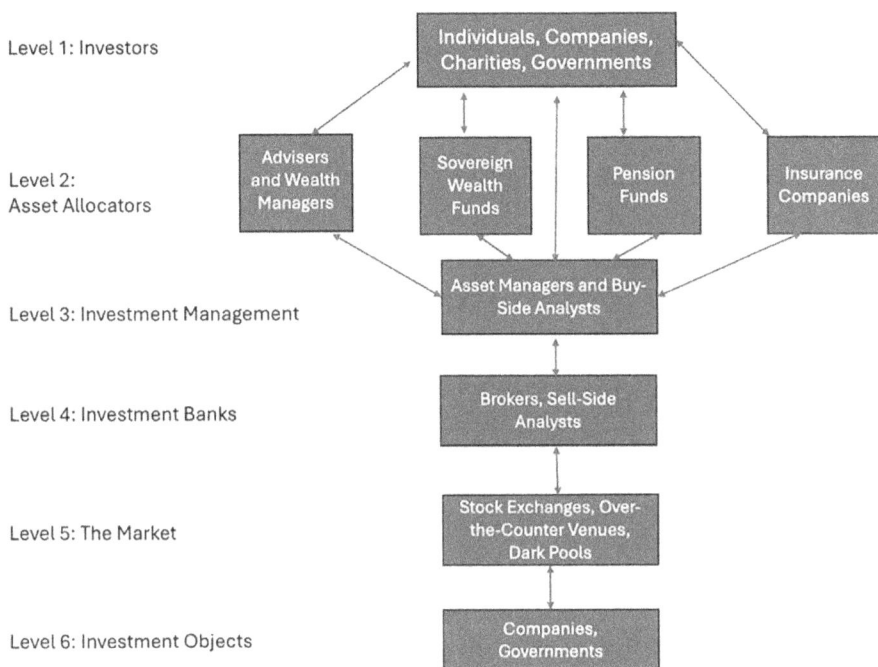

FIGURE 1.1 The investment chain.

Source: Adapted from Diane-Laure Arjaliès, Philip Grant, Iain Hardie, Donald A. MacKenzie, and Ekaterina Svetlova, *Chains of Finance: How Investment Management Is Shaped* (Oxford: Oxford University Press, 2017), x.

with other intermediaries. In other words, straight away there is intermediation upon the intermediation.

Having received advice from their investment consultants, the investment vehicles then allocate their assets (actually their clients' assets) to investment management firms at level 3. Here there is a wide variety of options in terms of the firms themselves as well as the specific funds within each firm that pursue different investment strategies. Two common strategies that we will discuss later are *long-only mutual funds*, which pursue buy-and-hold strategies, possibly on the basis of value or growth criteria or both; and *long/short hedge funds*, which seek to benefit not only from investing in firms whose stock prices will increase over time but also from betting against firms that they see as overvalued. Many other strategies exist, but these are among the most common and well established in financial markets.

Once the assets are allocated to investment management firms at level 3 of the investment chain, those firms take advice from other intermediaries, such as sell-side analysts working in research departments in investment banks, credit rating agencies, and industry/expert networks, in order to better inform themselves about the prospects of particular companies and industries in different parts of the world.

After deciding on which investment objects to allocate their assets to, investment management firms generally hire investment banks or brokerage firms at level 4 to execute the necessary trades (e.g., to buy or sell stocks and bonds or packaged products such as exchange-traded funds or index funds) via various trading venues, level 5 in the figure. These trading venues can be public stock exchanges such as the London Stock Exchange and the New York Stock Exchange or over-the-counter venues with more limited numbers of buyers and sellers. The money involved in these trades does not end up with the company, government, or investment object per se because what is described here is trading on the secondary market: i.e., investors are effectively trading among themselves. Ownership of a company's shares, for example, may change in the course of this process, but the balance sheets and income statements of said company grow or decline in a somewhat parallel universe to all this secondary trading of their shares.

This is a rather simplified and stylized illustration of how investment management generally operates via the investment chain.[2] Yet even in this simplified illustration, we can see myriad groups of financial intermediaries playing a part in allocating the assets of the initial investors to various investment objects. Because many people are trying to get their own slice of the pie, it is no surprise that financial intermediation is a huge economic sector in its own right. Indeed, the financial sector now constitutes around 12 percent of GDP in OECD countries.[3] Arjaliès et al. suggest that it is far from clear that this has been beneficial for countries, for individual savers, or for the quality of investment decisions. Indeed, related research demonstrates that the unit cost of financial intermediation has not declined since the 1880s in spite of technological improvements to systems and processes. Instead, the economic benefit of technological improvements has been captured by senior financial intermediaries in the form of higher pay.[4] Critical interpretations suggest that costly financial intermediation is less a price worth paying for access to financial markets and more a tax on the rest of the economy, slowing its growth and imposing unnecessary financial penalties on savers, investors, consumers, and citizens more broadly. Note that we do not limit our constituencies here to investors because even those who are not explicitly or consciously making investment decisions will find that their economic fates are tied up in financial markets whether they like it or not, either as purchasers of insurance products (providing the money that is reinvested by insurance companies) or as citizens who simply live in a society where wealth distribution is skewed by processes of financial intermediation.[5]

One of the more high-profile criticisms of the investment chain in recent years has been directed at level 4 and the persistence of *active* asset managers in charging high fees to try to "beat the market," something that study after study and widely available industry metrics illustrate they consistently fail to do. This is one reason that in recent years many investors have turned to *passive* funds, which (1) don't try to beat the market but rather invest in all or a specific segment of the market in an attempt to reproduce average market returns and (2) charge fees that are multiples lower than those charged by active fund managers.

Active funds have lost a seismic amount of market share to passive or index funds in recent years. According to the Investment Company Institute, the swing from active to passive management in the United States alone since 2013, captured in figure 1.2, has amounted to $4.8 trillion.[6] However, the global percentage of assets under active management remains above 60 percent, according to Morningstar.[7] This suggests that despite overwhelming evidence that passive or index funds outperform their active counterparts, the asset allocation industry (level 2) continues to place a significant portion of the assets entrusted to it with high-fee, low-performance fund managers.

The persistence of underperforming financial intermediaries is a curious one—in particular because the cultural imaginaries associated with capital markets conjure up images of freewheeling, dynamic traders hungrily exploiting anomalies and arbitrage

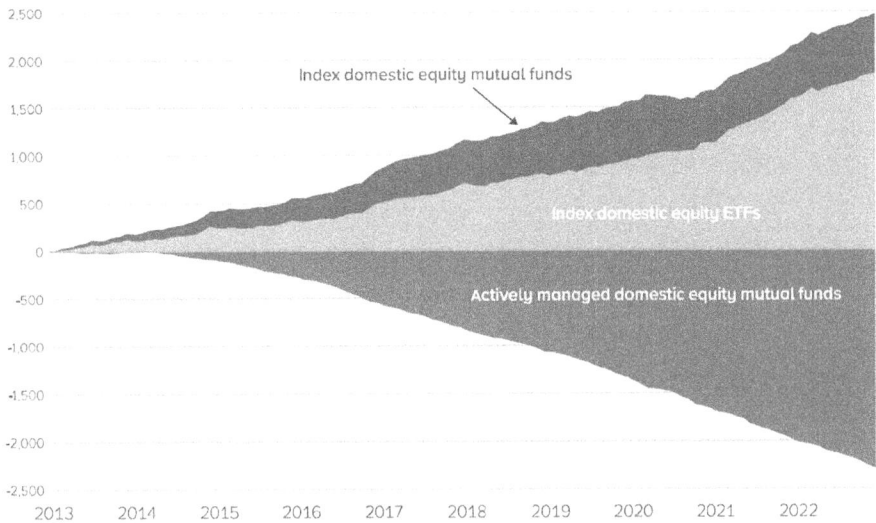

Index domestic equity mutual funds

Index domestic equity ETFs

Actively managed domestic equity mutual funds

2,500
2,000
1,500
1,000
500
0
-500
-1,000
-1,500
-2,000
-2,500

2013 2014 2015 2016 2017 2018 2019 2020 2021 2022

FIGURE 1.2 Cumulative flows from actively managed domestic equity mutual funds to index domestic equity mutual funds and index domestic equity ETFs (billions of dollars, monthly).

Source: Investment Company Institute, *2023 Investment Company Fact Book* (Washington, DC: Investment Company Institute, 2023), 48, https://www.icifactbook.org /pdf/2023-factbook.pdf.

opportunities. Markets, we are told, are largely efficient, so we shouldn't expect there to be a place for those who routinely provide overpriced, underperforming services. And yet there is.

THE BUY-SIDE AND THE SELL-SIDE

Our objective in this book is not to explore all aspects of financial intermediation that are captured in figure 1.1. An overview of this has already been offered by Arjaliès et al. Rather, we focus specifically on levels 3 and 4 of the investment chain in an attempt to understand the dynamics between those who work in investment management firms (known in the industry as the buy-side because they buy services from other intermediaries around them) and those who work in equity research divisions (known in the industry as sell-side analysts because they are effectively selling advisory and execution services to the buy-side).

Indeed, an alternative depiction of how the buy-side and sell-side interact is offered in the flow diagram in figure 1.3. This diagram identifies some of the important factors in the complex interactions between these two different groups, which are not generally explored by existing academic research. Here we can see that the sell-side analysts are positioned in a key brokerage

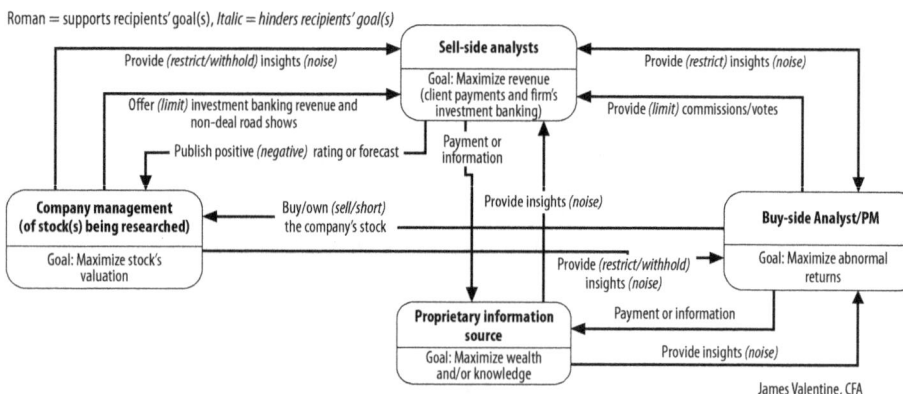

FIGURE 1.3 An alternative depiction of how the buy-side and sell-side interact.

role between their buy-side clients and the investment objects of those clients. The sell-side research team putatively offers key insights to the buy-side on the financial prospects of companies, which they glean through a mixture of company-specific research, industry analysis, and relationships and insights they cultivate directly with the management of companies in which their buy-side clients do, or might wish to, invest.

The sell-side thus operates in between two key groups of actors in the investment chain, a situation not fully captured in the previous work of Arjaliès et al. These relationships are further complicated by the institutional reality of sell-side analysts, which both enables and constrains their activity, as captured by the red and green labels in figure 1.3. It is also worth noting that sell-side analysts tend not to work as stand-alone entities, although some boutique research firms do exist. Rather, sell-side research is generally the responsibility of a department or division within an investment bank. Figure 1.4 offers a broad depiction of how investment banks are often formally structured.

We can see from figure 1.4 that research is just one aspect of what an investment bank does. Another key aspect is the trading of stocks. This denotes the execution aspects of buying and selling shares, which investment management firms tend to subcontract out. The bank's sell-side researchers recommend stocks to their buy-side clients, who may well act on their advice and decide to buy stocks through the capital markets division of the same investment bank, generating more commissions for the investment bank in question. Indeed, historically, sell-side research has been paid for indirectly via the commissions that

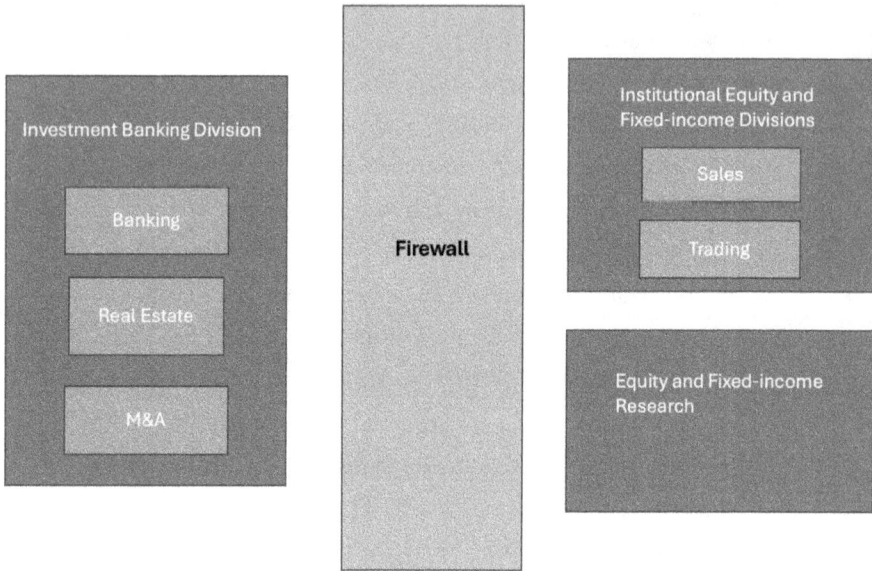

FIGURE 1.4 Typical investment bank structure.

it generates. The potential for conflicts of interest here is high, however, as more trading activity means more fees earned by the investment bank, even though more trading activity might not necessarily be in the best interests of its buy-side clients.

Beyond capital markets services, investment banks engage in what is known as *corporate finance* or (confusingly and unhelpfully) *investment banking activity*. This involves providing services directly to companies that wish to engage with the financial markets to raise capital through either an initial public offering or a secondary share issue, furnishing them with due diligence advisory services regarding mergers and acquisitions, finding buyers for their newly issued bonds, etc. This means buy-side firms are clients of investment banks for research and for stock transactions, and corporations in need of capital or advice on mergers and acquisitions are clients of investment banking *divisions* within these investment banks. Again, the opportunity for conflicts of interest here is quite broad, which is why legislation in most contexts insists on there being *fire-walls* between the various functions of the investment bank, although our research has found the effectiveness of such walls is routinely called into question. In addition, investment banks might have their own asset management divisions—effectively their own investment management firms—so they are involved in myriad activities that have become institutionalized features of professional investing. The relationships between sell-side analysts and their buy-side clients are at the heart of these activities.

While the sell-side is a catchall term for a range of different activities performed by investment banks, the buy-side also has its complexity, split up among heads of investment who oversee different funds or even funds of funds,[8] portfolio managers, and the various analysts who work for them. For the purposes of the present book, we focus on those with whom sell-side analysts interact directly—namely, the portfolio managers who run specific active funds and the various analysts who work for them. Sell-side analysts routinely present investment ideas to both of these buy-side groups. Indeed, in many respects, all of these actors do quite similar jobs, analyzing companies and their prospects, although portfolio managers are the only ones with ultimate responsibility for trading decisions.

Sell-side Analysts	Buy-side Analysts
• Focuses on niche sectors and provides reports on company financials	• Covers multiple sectors, following more companies than sell-side analysts
• May place "buy", "sell" and "hold" recommendations on company stocks	• Combines their own research with that of the sell-side
• Provides useful information to the buy side	• Identifies potential negative outcomes for investors to avoid
• Brings in new business when predictions are proven right	• Helps investors identify which sell-side analysts are the most valuable

FIGURE 1.5 Sell-side versus buy-side analysts.

Buy-side and sell-side analysts are very similar: both generally perform fundamental analysis of a company's financial accounts while incorporating other forms of industry analysis and nuggets of unique insight garnered from idiosyncratic sources in order to arrive at what they hope is a more accurate value of a stock than the market price.[9] The differences between buy-side and sell-side analysts, at least in terms of their ostensible, commonly understood roles, are well captured in figure 1.5, which summarizes information from the website of the Chartered Financial Analysts Society (CFAS; the main industry body for both buy-side and sell-side analysts). As the figure shows, both sets of analysts are presumed to perform roles that are geared primarily to provide investment recommendations to portfolio managers, with sell-side analysts focusing on a smaller, specialized pool of stocks and buy-side analysts taking a broader view, funneling and filtering the ideas of sell-side analysts to present to their portfolio managers.

HOW ANALYSTS SPEND THEIR TIME

Given that analysts appear to be the go-betweens connecting investment managers and other key players in the investment industry, focusing in more detail on what they do and how they spend their time should reveal more about the different types of practices and interactions that take place in the investment industry more broadly. For this, we refer to the industry competency model (figure 1.6), taken from

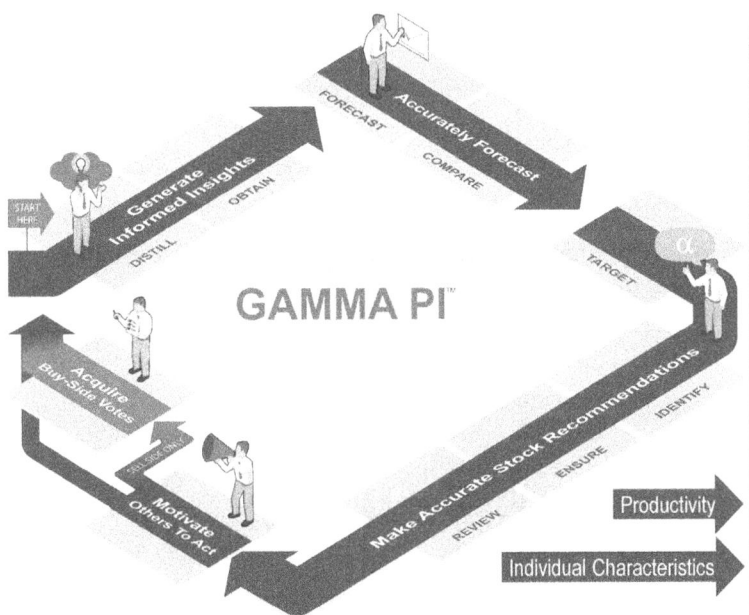

FIGURE 1.6 The GAMMA PI industry competency model.

Source: analystsolutions.com.

a well-known training company for sell-side analysts, Ana-lystSolutions. The GAMMA PI model has been built from industry research on buy-side and sell-side analysts' daily tasks (its name derives from the first letter of each stage in the figure).

While value may be in the eye of the beholder, the stated goal for most money managers on the buy-side is to generate excess returns, which, the widely held argument goes, is more likely to occur when those managers have better insights than the overall market. Analysts who focus on those activities that provide them this information asymmetry tend to find themselves in higher demand than those who simply repeat the consensus or company management views. Focusing in more detail on this industry-derived depiction of analysts' daily tasks, we can distinguish between what the analyst industry considers to be higher-value and lower-value versions of each particular task in order to throw into relief what analysts actually do on a day-to-day basis.

GENERATE INFORMED INSIGHTS

- *Lower value*: Analysts spend a considerable proportion of their days in a "discovery" phase, where they distill macro, industry, and company information to identify the most important factors likely to influence stock valuations. In the initial lower-value phase of this process, "getting up to speed," they are likely to use publicly available information, which is table stakes, when researching a stock. Their activities include

- Participating in widely publicized conference calls/ meetings/field trips arranged by others (e.g., quarterly conference calls),
- Reading company regulatory filings/press releases to get a general understanding of the company and its performance, and
- Reviewing news or other widely disseminated, publicly available data.

• *Higher value*: Analysts focusing on generating excess returns take a further step by seeking information asymmetry through building a network of informed and accurate information sources to identify and validate their views about the factors likely to influence their stocks. Their activities include

- Holding private, one-on-one meetings with management of the competitors of the stock being researched (private and publicly traded competitors),
- Reaching out to unique information sources (e.g., privately held company/industry consultants), and
- Conducting proprietary surveys.

ACCURATELY FORECAST

• *Lower value*: Analysts generate a financial forecast(s) similar to consensus or company guidance. Their activities include

- Updating financial forecast models (in Excel) based on company-provided data or guidance and
- Making minor updates and adjustments to financial forecasts based on new public information.

- *Higher value*: Analysts generate a financial forecast(s) more accurate than consensus by using unique insights not held by consensus. Their activities include
  - Updating financial forecast models (in Excel) based on unique or proprietary analysis around a factor that will likely be material to the stock's valuation,
  - Validating out-of-consensus financial forecasts with informed, nonbiased information sources, and
  - Conducting scenario analysis to stress-test financial forecasts.

MAKE ACCURATE STOCK RECOMMENDATIONS

- *Lower value*: Analysts use a single valuation method—which is also the most conventional method—with a stock's current valuation assumptions in creating a price target similar to consensus.
- *Higher value*: Analysts apply multiple valuation methods—which are also the most appropriate methods—with a stock's current valuation assumptions in creating a price target(s) more accurate than consensus. Their activities include
  - Adjusting forecasts or valuation methods to ensure the companies within a sector are comparable,
  - Analyzing historical and current valuation parameters for a stock to correctly forecast the future price target,
  - When making stock recommendations, developing a range of price targets (upside, downside, base case), and

- When making stock recommendations, valuing the stock by more than one method.
- *Higher value*: Analysts identify the optimal time to purchase or sell a stock (not too early or too late). Their activities include
  - Before making a major change in stock recommendations, assessing market sentiment,
  - Researching elements of risk rather than only the upside for high-conviction stock calls, and
  - Identifying why any out-of-consensus financial forecasts differ from consensus forecasts.

MOTIVATE OTHERS TO ACT (COMMUNICATIONS)

- Lower-value and higher-value activities for this area result in the same output mediums (reports, presentations, phone calls), but the content differs significantly.
- *Lower value*: Analysts prepare and deliver stock communications that are similar to consensus or company management.
- *Higher value*: Analysts follow the ADViCE framework, which is based on how portfolio managers prefer to consume research:
  - Aware: Make others aware of alternative scenarios and views as well as adjustments to their theses.
  - Differentiated: Explain how their views differ from the consensus thinking about the stock and its catalyst(s).
  - Validated: Support their key points with independent research.

- Conclusion oriented: Be conclusive about their stock ratings and catalysts.
- Easy to consume: Make the communication easy for others to consume.

ACQUIRE BUY-SIDE VOTES (FOR SELL-SIDE ANALYSTS ONLY)

- Analysts create research and events that are valued by their clients on topics not being discussed by others in the financial market or media.
- Analysts identify and build relationships with new clients likely to provide profitable contributions. Their activities include
  - Calling or meeting with clients to communicate their research insights,
  - Hosting conferences and field trips that their buy-side clients find valuable, and
  - Preparing for and presenting at their sales force meeting(s).

This depiction and associated descriptions of the daily tasks of buy-side and sell-side analysts draw on one of the authors' thirty-year immersion in the field as variously a sell-side analyst, the head of research in an investment bank, and the owner of an analyst training company. However, during this thirty-year period, an increasing disjunction between what sell-side analysts are ostensibly hired to do and what they are valued for by asset and money managers on the buy-side has become apparent. While many analysts spend huge amounts of time generating earnings forecasts and stock recommendations, recent academic research, both by ourselves[10] and by others, suggests that asset managers do not primarily seek these from their analysts. Instead, results from a survey presented by Lawrence Brown et al. suggest that asset managers value analysts for their in-depth industry knowledge and ability to broker access to company management rather than their soothsaying abilities.[11]

The main insights from this survey are presented in table 1.1. The CFAS does not mention the brokering of access to company management as one of the roles of sell-side analysts even though this ranks second on the list of survey responses. The CFAS does, however, continue to train and certify those seeking the coveted CFA designation primarily on the basis of

TABLE I.I Results of a survey asking how useful the following sell-side services are to buy-side analysts

Service	Average rating
1. Industry knowledge	5.04
2. Management access	4.70
3. Calls and visits you initiate with sell-side analysts	3.91
4. Written reports	3.76
5. Knowledge of other investors' opinions or holdings	3.43
6. Calls and visits sell-side analysts initiate with you	2.71
7. Earnings forecasts	2.67
8. Stock recommendations	1.76

Source: Adapted from Lawrence D. Brown, Andrew C. Call, Michael B. Clement, and Nathan Y. Sharp, "The Activities of Buy-Side Analysts and the Determinants of Their Stock Recommendations," *Journal of Accounting and Economics* 62, no. 1 (2016), 147.

services ranked fourth, seventh, and eighth on the list of survey responses. As such, we conclude that there is a serious mismatch between financial analysts' ostensible, institutionalized activities and their actual activities (which are also the primary source of their value). Consequently, there is a need for more in-depth anthropological understandings of what analysts do and what impacts and consequences are generated by their myriad interactions with other market participants.

CONCLUSION

In this chapter, we have introduced the institutional context within which our key protagonists operate in the hope that this will help the reader who is not well acquainted with these particular links in the investment chain. The financial intermediaries that we focus on in this book—asset managers and analysts on both the buy-side and the sell-side—operate within a field that is undergoing disruption and change, as characterized by asset flows out of active fund management and into passive fund management. Against this backdrop, we have explained the key ostensible functions of equity research intermediaries and highlighted the functions for which these intermediaries are valued, pointing out that these two sets of functions are not necessarily the same. In chapter 2, we will drill down further into what we see as the key conceptual tensions in our effort to make sense of these financial intermediaries, and in doing so, we will highlight in greater depth why we believe a whole book devoted to understanding what they do is worthwhile.

Chapter Two

SOCIAL STRUCTURES OF FINANCIAL MARKETS

A sophisticated economic sociology will neither throw the valuable corpus of economic reasoning out the window, nor be so seduced by it as to produce a "rational choice" argument that loses touch with the classical sociological tradition; rather, it will seek to understand how modern economics can be integrated with a social constructionist account of economic institutions, and what the division of labor must therefore be between sociology and economics.

—Marc Granovetter, "Economic Institutions as Social Constructions"

DOMINANT FRAMES OF FINANCIAL MARKETS/INTERMEDIARIES

Existing academic literature on financial intermediaries offers both a lot and a little. It offers much, for example, in terms of hundreds, if not thousands, of studies on sell-side equity analysts alone, and it pays a lot of attention to how the predictions and forecasts in their published reports turn out to be more or less accurate.[1] This academic obsession with the sell-side's soothsaying abilities is curious because, as we pointed out in chapter 1, participants in capital markets are not particularly interested in these predictions and forecasts.[2] We try to avoid this scholastic fallacy here by focusing on what investment professionals identify as interesting, valuable, and important. Existing research is of little help to us in this endeavor because, in contrast to the vast quantities of print devoted to the sell-side's powers of prediction, there is much less published academic work on fund managers or anyone from the buy-side. In this regard, existing research is both lopsided and problematically wrapped up in an epistemic doxa[3] of its own construction, focusing on what it can readily measure rather than what substantively matters.

In one sense, the voluminous academic literature on financial intermediaries suggests a belief in their importance to financial markets. Indeed, a dominant thesis on equity analysts is that they are effective in discovering, interpreting, and disseminating information—in summary, they are important *information* intermediaries.[4] The word *information* here has a specific tenor in that it is presumed to be materially relevant: i.e., it will impact an expert actor's perception or valuation of a particular company stock. This can be contrasted with *noise*, which does not contain material information, although naive retail traders might act on it in any case because, as many scholars presume, such traders are unable to tell the difference.[5] Financial intermediaries such as analysts, although not perfect, are generally presumed to be intermediations of information rather than noise.

Orthodox literature on financial intermediaries offers little in terms of conceptual breadth, relying on an intellectual framework that frequently leads to confounding results. Almost everything published on financial intermediaries is couched within the frame of neoclassical economics, which presumes, among other things, that economic agents are rational, individualistic utility maximizers. Relatedly, according to this framework, sell-side actors are believed both to communicate critically useful information to decision makers (e.g., there are supply chain bottlenecks in the pool pump industry that will impact production for the next six months) and to bias their predictions whenever it is advantageous to do so.[6]

Thus, while much research on financial intermediaries points out instances where equity analysts fail to perfectly process certain types of information in a timely manner,[7] these instances are viewed as exceptions that prove the rule that these analysts are important and necessary players in financial markets. Those adhering to this dominant intellectual framework surrounding financial intermediaries do not appear to be very aware of this tension. Indeed, after presenting various arguments in this book to different audiences at different universities over the last few years, we have concluded that attachment to these main tenets of neoclassical economics is tantamount to something of an unshakeable commitment. For example, questioning the efficiency of markets by suggesting that many financial intermediaries persist while seemingly providing little or even negative value to their clients or that financial intermediaries might not always improve corporate governance has elicited some fairly vehement responses from colleagues over the years, particularly those working in accounting and finance departments in business schools.

We believe these responses have less to do with the particular evidence or empirical results we are presenting than they do with the conceptual implications of our arguments. In essence, exploring how financial markets seem to tolerate ideas and individuals who don't always add value implicitly challenges the widely held notion that "economics really does constitute the universal grammar of social science."[8]

We contend that economics alone cannot offer satisfactory explanations for why the chain of financial intermediation[9] behaves in the way that it does. As implied earlier, this is curious because it is the economics-based literature that gives rise to the paradox that motivated us to write this book in the first place: financial intermediaries are widely criticized for their want of accuracy and utility, yet they persist as important actors in financial markets. Without the emergence of an academic subindustry devoted to documenting how fund managers underperform benchmarks[10] and how equity analysts are both incentivized to generate trading volume[11] and often quite inaccurate in their predictions for a number of reasons,[12] we wouldn't have an intellectual knot to untangle. Indeed, even more ecumenical economic framings of financial intermediaries struggle to fully explain their persistence in financial markets, as we will see when we consider behavioral approaches to understanding finance.

ECONOMICS 2.0 AND 3.0: BEHAVIORAL AND SOCIAL FINANCE

Behavioral finance supplements the economic framing of traditional finance with a dose of cognitive psychology, drawing heavily on the work of early pioneers such as Daniel Kahneman and Amos Tversky.[13] This leads to a focus on individual-level cognitive biases, as is explained by David Hirshleifer (NB: not Jack Hirshleifer, who made the outlandish claims about economics being the universal grammar of social science that we mentioned earlier): "Since people need to make judgments and decisions quickly using limited cognitive resources, they necessarily use shortcuts, often called 'heuristics.' All thinking builds upon cognitive algorithms that operate automatically below the level of consciousness. The term 'heuristics' encompasses both innate and automatic processes, and learned or consciously selected rules of thumb."[14]

These heuristics are associated with a series of different cognitive biases, attitudes, or behaviors that the behavioral finance canon has been at pains to document and provide evidence for over the past three decades. These biases include overconfidence, overoptimism, distorted framing, self-confirmation bias, loss aversion, information neglect, the disposition effect, the reverse disposition effect, reinforcement learning, overextrapolation, the sunk cost fallacy, in-group bias, ambiguity aversion, and status quo bias.

This smorgasbord of biases has been incredibly helpful in painting a picture of financial markets as populated by human beings as they are more readily recognizable: i.e., as people with flaws and foibles rather than as the rather fantastical omniscient, perfect information processors that are supposed by certain branches of economics.[15] If people are flawed in how they process information, then prices will not reflect all available information, and markets will therefore be, at least to some extent, inefficient. In this regard, behavioral finance has significantly altered our understanding of financial markets and of financial intermediaries.

However, there remain a number of limitations and problems with behavioral finance. First, most behavioral finance research draws on data from laboratory studies, with the subjects often MBA students who happen to be hanging around business schools at the time and who have had limited experience working in financial fields. Even when experimental designs do enlist investment professionals, they still don't effectively mirror real-life conditions. Second, behavioral studies tend to ignore the affective realm of feelings, which are harder to map or capture in experimental designs but which nevertheless have been shown to impact investment decisions in major ways.[16] Third, the psychological focus of behavioral studies privileges analysis of the micro, cognitive level of individuals, while downplaying or completely ignoring the social and institutional factors that potentially give rise to their biases, attitudes, and behaviors in the first place. Behavioral studies occasionally are cognizant of this lack of attention to social structures, prompting calls for studies to explore group dynamics and social context in more detail.[17]

All of these limitations are well recognized by David Hirshleifer, who consequently has called for a move beyond behavioral finance to what he labels *social finance*. Social finance denotes the study of the structure of social interactions, how financial ideas spread and evolve, and how social processes affect financial outcomes.[18] Additionally such an enterprise would "draw on social psychology and sociology as well as cognitive psychology and decision theory, and will require focused attention to the microstructure of social transactions."[19] In his 2020 presidential address to the American Finance Association, he hailed social finance as a "once in a generation research opportunity" and "a new way to understand human behavior."[20]

Beyond a general cri de coeur, Hirshleifer doesn't offer much in the way of specifics for a social finance research program, although he does suggest that a key building block of social finance is *social transmission bias*—a directional shift in signals or ideas induced by social transactions—in analytical frameworks.[21] This usefully draws attention to the ways in which economic behavior is socially emergent—the product of network interactions: e.g., Hirshleifer points out how investors have been shown to change their trading strategies after speaking to other investors. However, this does tend to reduce the entire social context to one new novel form of bias for us to add to the behavioral canon.

Irrespective of whether Hirshleifer goes far enough or not, the implications of his social finance argument are clear in terms of the theories and methods that should be applied to make sense of financial intermediaries and other economic actors. In terms of the former, we need to take a broader social science view rather than relying on the behavioral cocktail of economics with a dose of cognitive psychology. Religion, ideology, gender, culture, and education are all phenomena that the sociological tool kit can bring to bear in explaining economic action. In terms of the latter, information about how financial intermediaries actually behave and why cannot readily be gleaned from models derived from experiments but rather must come from observing and speaking firsthand to both those who make investment decisions and those who advise them.

SOCIAL STRUCTURES

David Hirshleifer's welcome admonishment of his economics and finance colleagues was very naive in one regard because economic sociologists had arrived at this conclusion several decades prior. Indeed, one of the fathers of modern sociology, Max Weber, published *The Protestant Ethic and the Spirit of Capitalism* in 1905, arguing clearly that the foundations for economic action were social in nature, turning Karl Marx's base-superstructure argument—where economics determines social relations—on its head.

Throughout the twentieth century, a number of other works have demonstrated the social foundations of economic activity. For example, Pierre Bourdieu is probably most famous for his 1979 work *La Distinction*, which explores the importance of cultural capital to the class structure in late twentieth-century France. However, his key work on economic sociology—*The Social Structures of the Economy*—does very effectively what its title suggests. Taking the seemingly mundane arena of the French housing market, he situates economic decision-making within the perspective of a historically constituted field that is constantly being mobilized, along with its attendant cultural norms and congealed social and institutional networks, in order to both constrain and enable what seem, on the surface, to be relatively unremarkable decisions about, say, what kind of house a newly married couple will realistically aspire to buy on the outskirts of Paris. Among other targets in this book, he takes a swipe at the notion of rational economic man and at neoclassical economic theory for their "postulates lacking any anthropological underpinning"[22] and for their inability to take structural effects into account when proffering explanations of individual decision-making.

Instead of the market, where an abstract logic of mechanical, automatic, and instantaneous determination of prices prevails, Bourdieu advances a notion of a field in which the dispositions and decisions of individual actors are not atomized or free-floating but are couched in the social networks and cultural norms immanent to these actors' organizations and institutional conditions. We suggest that any proper analysis of the behavior of financial intermediaries needs to adopt a similar sensibility. In this regard, we follow Bourdieu's insight that "it is not prices that determine everything, but everything that determines prices"[23] and focus on the "everything" that surrounds financial calculations rather than the calculations themselves, as so many accounting and finance scholars unfortunately do when they take their unit of analysis to be a rate of return, an earnings forecast, or some other such variable.

Bourdieu's huge influence on late-twentieth- and early-twenty-first-century sociology notwithstanding, his impact specifically on economic sociology has been more muted. Indeed, recent calls to bring his conception of field + habitus to the fore to remedy some of the deficiencies of behavioral economics/finance by illustrating how social (field) and mental (habitus) structures constitute one another[24] are indicative of a theoretical potential that has yet to be fully explored. There have, of course, been scattered applications of Bourdieu's economic sociology to various financial fields. For example, his work has been used to make sense of the world of wealth managers, where we learn about the appropriate dispositions, cultural pursuits, and social capital that these individuals need to cultivate in order to be accepted as trusted consiglieri by ultra-high-net-worth individuals.[25] Others have used Bourdieusian ideas to elucidate the hidden rules of the game in career advancement in financial services,[26] showing also how these rules can vary across different geographical and cultural contexts.[27] Bourdieu has also been helpful in our understanding of the financial reasoning of financial traders, in particular pointing toward the different aesthetic judgments that traders make to justify certain trading approaches (e.g., statistical arbitrage) over others (e.g., chartist analysis).[28] His impact on understanding asset management though has been very limited, with only one Edinburgh-based study (to our knowledge) devoted to understanding both the habitus and the social structures that pertain to the fund management field.[29] Given the economic importance of fund management, more work is needed that explores both the mental and the social structures that make up this field.

SOCIAL NETWORKS

At a broad level, this focus on the social structures of economic action has much in common with the work of another major economic sociologist of the twentieth century, Marc Granovetter. Like Bourdieu, Granovetter takes issue with the utilitarian approach in neoclassical economics, which "assumes rational, self-interested behavior affected minimally by social relations."[30] This leads to an implausibly "undersocialized view" of economic behavior. Equally, however, Granovetter takes aim at other approaches in the social sciences that tend to take an "oversocialized" view of economic action, most commonly by adopting rather crude interpretations of Karl Polanyi's embeddedness argument, where all economic activity is reduced to a mere function of surrounding social structures.

Both the undersocialized and the oversocialized views, paradoxically perhaps, lead to an atomized view of human behavior. In the first instance, economic actors are free-floating, price-taking buyers and sellers with perfect information seeking to maximize their own utility. In the second instance, economic actors are reduced to unthinking drones who behave in accordance with their prescribed roles. In both cases, the immediate context in which actors operate is presumed not to matter. In order to avoid either of these conceptual extremes, the middle-ground positions that are broadly shared by Bourdieu and Granovetter offer a way forward. Both point toward the importance of analyzing economics actors in the context of "concrete, ongoing systems of social relations."[31]

For such an enterprise, we need to examine the premise that each economic field—whether a field is an investment bank, the community of active fund management, stock exchanges, or even financial markets—is socially constructed. In particular, this implies that an economic field is not so much the outcome of a predictable market response to a particular problem, like a purely economic approach to, say, transaction costs, as it is a continuously developing set of social ties, conventions, and worldviews that interact with other societal lifeworlds. As such, because of their inherently emergent nature, economic fields should be understood not in relation to the supposed functions they fulfill but sui generis as social and cultural phenomena with rules that need to be deduced anthropologically by examining the behavior of their relevant actors. For example, we can look at the business groups in different countries (e.g., zaibatsus in Japan, chaebols in South Korea, and *grupos económicos* in Latin America) and see what are effectively "congealed social networks"[32] that evolve and operate dynamically in relation to the societies in which they exist.

Granovetter also offers the example of the U.S. electrical utility industry, which chose the path of centralized power stations rather than decentralized generators not because the latter were technologically superior or offered a functionally better solution but because their advocates were more adroit politically at generating support for their ideas. The persistence of the QWERTY keyboard similarly shows how certain practices and ways of doing things come to be locked in way beyond their having any practical usage.[33] It is tempting here to portray financial intermediaries as the human equivalent of the QWERTY keyboard, but that possibly does a disservice to the QWERTY keyboard, which at least was the answer to a particular mechanical problem at a point in time.

The key point here is that fields have idiosyncratic origins and take on a certain path dependency, whether because of political support, inertia, or associated developments from overlapping fields. In turn, path dependencies predetermine future courses of action and might even support the evolution of inherent contradictions (as we will see in the following chapters). As such, the persistence of ideas, practices, and actors in fields cannot be explained solely or even primarily in terms of functionality or a preexisting set of ideas, such as economic efficiency; rather, any explanation must also reference the "accretions of activity patterns around personal networks."[34]

SOCIAL FIELDS

We see that social structures matter in financial markets, as they do in any social field. Moreover, those social structures accrete via the conscious and unconscious actions of the individuals who populate the field. This brings us back to the importance of habitus + field as a central concept of economic sociology. Whereas *field* refers to a structured social space populated by agents whose positions in that social space can be explained by their differential possession and utilization of various resources (or "forms of capital" in Bourdieusian parlance), *habitus* refers to the system of engrained dispositions held by individuals that simultaneously integrates past experiences, acts as a matrix of perceptions, and constitutes the basis for action in infinitely diverse situations. Habitus and field are in a constant dialectic, with the one shaping the other and giving rise to various structured practices. Indeed, Bourdieu even encapsulated the relationship among these different elements in a concise formula: [(habitus) (capital)] + field = practice.

Therefore, in order to understand specific practices in financial markets, such as, say, a sell-side analyst offering a particular earnings forecast or setting up a non-deal road show (effectively a series of meetings with company managers) for buy-side clients, it is important to attend to the habitus of those undertaking those practices as well as the forms of capital that are at play when those practices are being performed, all within the context of field-specific relationships. For example, to make sense of the practice of a non-deal road show, we can try to infer something of the motivation and assumptions of the sell-side analyst, which would reveal something about their habitus. We are also interested in identifying the different forms of capital that are at play in the execution of this practice. Clearly, social capital is required in the brokering of meetings between two groups of actors; economic capital will ultimately change hands as well, as the sell-side analyst will expect compensation of some sort (either directly or indirectly) for brokering this meeting; and symbolic capital is also at stake because sell-side analysts who are good at generating corporate access tend to be receive votes from their buy-side clients in annual surveys that are used to help rank the sell-side. Field dynamics are also evident in trying to match actors with similar dispositions and forms of capital: e.g., certain types of homophily tend to emerge in fields that follow their own laws of development.

This example illustrates the kind of phenomena that would be identified and explored by a researcher interested in understanding how social structures shape economic action from a Bourdieusian perspective. However, as we noted earlier, such a perspective is not universally shared by economic sociologists. Indeed, looking more specifically at the now burgeoning literature on the sociology of finance, we can more readily discern the heavy influence of Michel Callon and Bruno Latour.

Those using this actor-network theory (ANT) perspective are also interested in social networks and the individuals who populate them, but their approach is quite different in many ways from that of Bourdieu or Granovetter. Specifically, ANT is attached to an object-oriented ontology, which places objects as central to the sociological enterprise. In practical terms, this means that the sociology of finance heavily privileges phenomena such as market devices,[35] the material[36] and informational[37] infrastructures surrounding trading and exchanges, and the physical spaces within which financial actors make purposeful decisions.[38]

The insights offered by these and other studies in recent years have reshaped how we understand finance and have helped flesh out a view of financial markets that highlights how economic action is increasingly mediated by technology. We do not want to underestimate the importance of this, and, indeed, we need to acknowledge that this focus on objects is largely missing from the frameworks of Bourdieu and Granovetter. In fact, in Bourdieu's case he famously laughed openly at Callon's ascribing of agency to the scallops that populate Saint-Brieuc Bay in northern France.[39] Whether or not scallops have agency or stones have feelings is not something we want to dwell on here, but we do recognize that our understanding of financial markets has been enriched by the recognition of the central role played by various technological objects therein, whether those objects are the cables and satellites used by high-frequency traders,[40] the hardware installed to automate stock exchanges,[41] or the algorithms employed in modern-day trading systems.[42]

However, ANT approaches such as these tend to be onto-logically flat,[43] giving little sense of who the winners and losers are in financial markets and generally, although not exclu-sively, ignoring wider issues of political economy.[44] Moreover, in practical terms a focus on socio-technical systems doesn't help us resolve our central conundrum: why certain financial intermediaries and their attendant practices persist in finan-cial markets despite widespread skepticism over their value relevance. That being said, the ANT perspective has taught us to be sensitive to the importance of objects as and when they appear to shape and reshape habitus and field. As such, a socio-technical sensibility is layered on top of our substantively Bourdieusian-Granovetterian framework.

ANT is therefore a fellow conceptual traveler for us in this book, certainly much more so than mainstream economics is. To resolve the central conundrum of the book, we need, first of all, to set aside the homespun nostrums of economics and stop treating financial markets as if they are immune to the social dynamics to which all other areas of social and economic life are subject. What is called for, second, is a theoretical approach that looks more comprehensively at the social dynamics and power struc-tures surrounding economic behavior. We therefore need to view the various arenas that constitute financial markets as social and cultural fields that are governed by routine, habit, and a gradual evolution and establishment of taken-for-granted conventions. By starting from such a premise, our analytical gaze turns not just to the immediate activities and behavior of financial inter-mediaries or to the nonhuman objects they interact with but also to the social reality and pressures that surround them.

EPISTEMIC SCHISMS

One facet of this reality surrounding financial markets and financial intermediaries is an intellectual one. Underpinning finance as a field of practice are beliefs among practitioners as well as academic researchers about what is the most appropriate financial epistemology. These foundational beliefs, or the epistemic doxa,[45] generate a debate around this question: Should financial markets be treated as an object of rational analysis and therefore one that can be forecast, or are they driven by forces that make them inherently unpredictable? This debate frames an early-onset schism in finance, rooted at the emergence of modern finance theory and continuing through the ascendance of financial markets and the explosive growth in recent decades of financial intermediaries.

Schisms within fields are to be expected, driven as they are by a divisive, agonistic logic[46] or a "war of everyone against everyone, that is universal competition."[47] In Bourdieu's account, knowledge-based fields are always the site of a "more or less unequal struggle between agents unequally endowed with [field-]specific capital."[48] Capital here refers to assets or resources that are generally cultural, social, or economic in nature.[49]

Financial intermediaries fall, very roughly, into two broad intellectual camps or two different epistemic regimes.[50] The passive camp, which was mostly academic to begin with, supported the dominance of the efficient market hypothesis (EMH), which claims, in simple terms, that all available information is already incorporated into market prices. As such, no one can consistently outperform the market or invest in a way that yields more than a risk-adjusted return. The active camp, which is larger and much more varied, provided apologies for, ignored, or outright challenged the EMH camp and stated that smart, sophisticated actors can outperform markets. Adherents to this view went ahead and developed a dazzling variety of analytical and trading strategies that have been studied by economic sociologists, including high-frequency trading,[51] statistical arbitrage,[52] chartism,[53] momentum trading,[54] and fundamental analysis.[55]

Although many advocates of these various strategies acknowledge at least some elements of EMH at their core, the active and passive camps still have irreconcilable differences. When each camp is reduced to a set of general guidelines for action, they point in diametrically opposed directions. While the passive/ EMH camp denies the possibility of beating the market and aims instead to replicate it, the active/beat-the-market camp focuses its efforts on developing forms of expertise and attendant social structures that are geared toward doing just that. To use equine metaphors, whereas the active camp seeks to identify which horse will be win the horse race ex ante and place a bet on that horse, the passive camp sees such a gamble as pure folly and instead places a bet on every horse in the race on the assumption that most will perform pretty well overall.

Importantly, while this schism at the heart of finance is recognized as a lived reality by practitioners, we see virtually no academic research that treats finance as a whole as a field of knowledge that operates in a deeply contested intellectual and practical terrain. One exception to this is the recent work of Scott James and Lucia Quaglia, who show how "epistemic contestation" between different groups of financial actors can lead to a certain inaction when it comes to regulatory change.[56] We aim to build upon this work here by looking beyond specific instances of regulatory failure and by developing a theory of a field where practitioners do not agree about the validity of the knowledge and expertise they wield on a daily basis.

This theory, which is built upon our empirical findings, looks at institutional investment as a field that is inherently political, as it is characterized by a continuous struggle for advantageous positioning in a space where individuals wield personal prestige, knowledge, and expertise as key positional resources. Invariably, this struggle will lead to divisions within the field, as evidenced by the emergence of different subfields or communities of actors who have different habitus and who occupy different positions therein.[57] Bourdieu suggests that these divisions often coalesce around the *dominant*, who adopt more orthodox epistemological positions that they seek to robustly defend, and the *dominated*, who adopt more heterodox intellectual positions: "Those who . . . more or less completely monopolize the [field]specific capital . . . are inclined to conservation strategies—those which, in the fields of production of cultural goods, tend to defend orthodoxy—whereas those least endowed with capital (who are often also the newcomers, and therefore generally the youngest) are inclined towards subversion strategies, the strategies of heresy. Heresy, heterodoxy . . . is what brings the dominant agents out of their silence and forces them to produce the defensive discourse of orthodoxy."[58]

Other ways of framing this battle between the dominant and the dominated are offered by Neil Fligstein and Doug McAdam, who see field competition as generally taking place between incumbents and various challenger groups.[59] For the purposes of this book, we can position the active investment community as incumbents whose epistemology, field position, and general relevance are called into question by a challenger in the form of the passive investment community. Additionally, the value of Fligstein and McAdam's approach is not simply a change in terminology but also a greater microlevel focus on the ways in which fields can be infinitely subdivided. While a classic Bourdieusian approach lends itself readily to analyzing the main schisms and divisions that fields are riven by, Fligstein and McAdam's "Russian dolls"[60] approach to fields permits simultaneous analysis of the multiple divisions and boundaries immanent in the various communities that populate those fields.

We see that fields are agonistic in nature and comprised of different communities that vie for both symbolic and material rewards, for both intellectual and (at least in the case of economic fields) economic supremacy. However, this does not mean that the best or most intellectually robust arguments will necessarily win. Indeed, one of the main motivations of this book is to explain the persistence of agents whose intellectual outputs in their field are routinely questioned. The different knowledge bases, or epistemic regimes, in evidence in our two communities are important in providing road maps whereby individuals can navigate successfully around the field, but it is important to note, following Granovetter's analysis of power plants, that one road map or community will not necessarily prevail over the other because of its scientific validity.

CONCLUSION

In the investment field, actors do not compete in terms of accuracy per se; rather, they compete for influence on decision-making. While the former is scientific/intellectual in nature, the latter is much more social. Accuracy may be one means by which influence can be garnered, but as we will see in subsequent chapters, those who bestow influence are not always interested in accuracy and, indeed, sometimes seek to stifle it in order to achieve other ends. In turn, savvy actors in the field who observe wider field dynamics are able to judge when accuracy is not called for, adjusting both their practices and the messages they send to wider field participants accordingly.

Chapter Three

SOCIAL STICKINESS

It is always a laborious operation to pull up the roots of habits that time has fixed and organized in us.

—Emile Durkheim, *The Division of Labor in Society*

The patterns of use and of relationships among [modern] economic units are determined by habit.

—Max Weber, *Economy and Society*

OUR FINDINGS indicate strong interdependence between different subgroups within the investment field. This points toward the importance of congealed networks in explaining the structure of the investment field and the behavior of its participants. Specifically, we find evidence of interpersonal and interorganizational interdependencies that maintain the structure of the field despite regulatory and economic changes aimed at disrupting these. Habit, routine, conflicts of interest, and general "stickiness" between individuals and between organizations all combine to provide an overall stability and inertia to the field. These serve to confirm the general importance of an analytical perspective that emphasizes the social structures surrounding economic activity and knowledge production.

HABIT

Many theoretical approaches used when analyzing financial markets, whether these approaches are rooted in philosophy, sociology, or economics, tend to overlook the roles played by both habit and routine in market behavior. In contrast to approaches rooted in notions of rational action, market actors don't spend all day every day calculating the outcomes of particular courses of action. To do so would be exhausting and completely unsustainable. Rather, in the course of engaging in everyday life, people rely on taken-for-granted conventions accumulated and crystalized through daily repetitions.[1] The accumulated experience that results from this provides a basis for understanding and action in markets.

As the opening quotes from Emile Durkheim and Max Weber suggest, habit was a key cornerstone in the development of sociology as a discipline, although it has been suggested that the notion of unreflexive action lost sociological popularity in the latter half of the twentieth century.[2] Pierre Bourdieu is certainly responsible for a revival of interest in the concept of habit, which he approaches obliquely through a theoretical arsenal that includes concepts such as illusio (to be taken in and seduced by the game one is playing),[3] doxa (the prereflexive belief that the way things are is the way they ought to be),[4] and habitus (an individual's schema of ingrained affective, cognitive, and corporeal dispositions).[5] We will delve deeper into these concepts in subsequent chapters. In the present chapter, we focus primarily on the social relations in the investment field that effectively structure it and then congeal over time, thereby providing a basis on which that field's specific illusio, doxa, and habitus develop.

Indeed, our respondents were very cognizant of the extent to which habit shaped their own practices and routines. For example, one routine feature of sell-side analysis is the publication of research on the companies and industries that analysts follow. This research can take the form of a brief commentary on a company's recent earnings updates, a more detailed analysis of its published financial results, or a deep dive into a whole industry sector. A common refrain among the buy-side is that the vast majority of published sell-side research on companies adds little to no value. This raises the question of why such research is produced in the first place. Drew, working in New York as a sell-side analyst for a bulge bracket investment bank, responded to this question directly:

> Tradition probably. I'm trying to think back to these conversations, and the crazy part is everyone recognizes it. Everyone recognizes that the majority of the things that you publish are just totally worthless. Earnings notes? Forget about it. Nobody reads that. Earnings preview? It's as much for you to get your model in line as it is for the clients. I don't know. So why is there so much? I don't know. Just legacy patterns that we've adopted over the years.

"Tradition" and "legacy patterns" speak directly to the centrality of habit and routine to financial intermediation. This quote from Drew aligns with views expressed by other sell-side analysts on the topic of perfunctory, largely unread analyst research. James, working in Chicago, suggested that "people are [characterized by] inertia more than anything else." Shaun, a junior sell-side analyst in New York, had been in his role for only two years and made a similar comment: "There are a lot of analysts who are stuck in their ways, kind of like old dogs that don't really want to change." Shaun then went on to express frustration that his boss insisted his team produce eighty-page reports when, in his experience, clients really wanted only a few sentences:

> They [older analysts] think this works the best and that's what's always worked for them. Perhaps they're not cognizant of a changing industry dynamic, and maybe I'm naive and I've only been in the industry for two years, so it's hard for a younger analyst to disagree with the guy who's been in industry for thirty years if he's been doing it this specific way for this amount of time.

Being in the field for decades, as Shaun indicates, helps to establish as taken for granted the notion that buy-side actors are interested in long research reports, while all the quotes here from sell-side analysts show that the buy-side has minimal interest in such reports. The production of unwieldy and largely unread reports is a phenomenon that appeared to cross the Atlantic, a situation attested to by Ashley, a sell-side analyst in London, although in this instance he provided an important reason for the production of reports, one that relates not to market information but to the social and economic structure of the field:

I think there's the belief that if you do go quiet [don't produce reports], you'll lose business . . . it's just the way things
have always been done, and no one has had like a serious
look at it. Yeah, it's . . . I think people are just afraid that if
they stop, they'll lose clients.

Ashley alluded to a rational set of anxieties (losing clients)
rooted in the desire to maintain the sell-side position vis-à-vis
existing and potential clients on the buy-side. Although we see
that many on the sell-side acknowledged that reports are mostly
left unread, the sell-side continues to produce reports, following
the unchecked convention that "maybe it's just the way things
have always been done." Additionally, Ashley's quote surfaces
the implicit belief that sell-side actors need to produce reports
so that buy-side actors do not forget about their existence and
remain ready to utilize their services if the right opportunity
arrives. Both reasons indicate the central importance of habit
and routine in the investment field. While it is tempting to be
critical of this, as habit and routine denote a degree of inertia in
a field that prides itself on dynamism and innovation, we should
also recognize that some degree of inertia is essential for any
field to operate. Without the stability provided by inertia, fields
would be in an unsustainable state of constant chaos. As outlined earlier, our key point here is not that inertia is necessarily a
surprise finding but that the social fields that make up financial
markets should not be seen as immune to the dynamics that
characterize other arenas in social and economic life. Moreover, the social structures within which financial intermediaries

operate have an important effect on the content of the knowledge they produce, as we will discuss later.

LONG-TERM INTERPERSONAL TIES

Rationality-related approaches such as those emanating from behavioral finance tend to explain habit, routine, and inertia as being rooted in cognition: i.e., individuals simply follow existing conventions, and in so doing, they fail to consider or reflect on potentially more valuable ways of doing things, such as not writing reports that go unread. However, as argued earlier, behavioral finance's penchant for focusing primarily on the cognitive biases and fallacies of individuals offers only a limited explanation for such behavior. We argue that the existence of inertia in the field of investment advice, while having a cognitive dimension, should also be understood as rooted in the social structures of the surrounding field. Habitus and field are mutually constitutive.

An abundance of insights in this regard was proffered by our respondents, who repeatedly highlighted areas of interdependence between the career trajectories of the buy-side and the sell-side. Many of our interviewees described years-long, even decades-long, social and business ties that facilitated their professional activities. While this sentiment was expressed more by sell-side respondents than buy-side respondents, both groups expressed similar ideas regarding the importance of such ties for the field.

For example, Dylan, a junior buy-side analyst in Chicago, was relatively fresh out of college and had been in the industry for less than twelve months when we met him. Tapping into the freshness of his experience, we asked what had surprised him the most since starting his job:

> It's more of a people business than I had anticipated. Relationships really matter, both with the sell side, with corporates. I guess the idea in my head was that it was more of you just sit at a screen and read all day and do some calculations in Excel.

Academic research tends to portray sell-side analysts primarily as producers of quantitative outputs such as financial forecasts,[6] price targets,[7] and stock ratings,[8] key metrics that their buy-side clients ostensibly focus on in order to make buy, sell, and hold decisions about particular stocks. In other words, researchers presume the expertise of analysts is very cognitive and technocratic and pay little attention to the context within which these actors operate. However, we find that the production of analysts' quantitative outputs, as well as other aspects of the professional lives of actors in the field, has an important interpersonal component, which Dylan alluded to and for which he felt business school hadn't prepared him. This viewpoint was expressed by more seasoned respondents as well. For example, sell-side analysts mentioned that they had "developed relationships" (Danny, Chicago) with buy-side clients and that good interpersonal relations were important to success. Comments such as the following from Nathan, who had spent time working in both Chicago and New York, are indicative of this view. Here he was talking about traveling with buy-side clients to conferences or company visits:

If along the way I'm hanging out with the PM [portfolio manager] from [a buy-side shop], then that is a very important contact, right? That endears me to them. And I have their ear and again, to the extent that increasingly the business is about capturing mind share . . .

The implication here is that "capturing mind share" is not something that will come about if they merely produce good analysis, although this is seen as a baseline for many analysts in the field. Rather, Nathan suggested that interpersonal work needs to be undertaken to create the right social conditions in which such analysis can be communicated. "Hanging out" in a more social scenario generates endearment and renders the portfolio manager more susceptible to listening to what the sell-side analyst has to say. This resonates with social theories that highlight how important face-to-face communication is in increasing trust levels between individuals.[9]

Others emphasized that they needed to "carefully cultivate and maintain" relationships to support the business (Eric, New York, sell-side) and that "it takes time and effort" to develop these (Reuben, Chicago, buy-side, ex-sell-side). In general, relationships are maintained through routine phone conversations and further strengthened through planned, recurring social events such as meals, where sell-side and buy-side actors interact in a more relaxed fashion and where small talk and then shop talk follow.

The social structure of the field enables its continuity but also affects the content of the information and the quality of knowledge produced. Although many sell-side analysts saw good financial analysis as a necessary but insufficient condition for professional success, others viewed the prevalence of strong social ties between different financial intermediaries as a reason for the persistence of underperforming sell-side analysts in the marketplace. For example, George, working in Chicago as a portfolio manager for a global asset manager, had almost twenty years of experience. He suggested that "85 percent of sell-side analysts add no or insignificant value to buy-side investment decisions." In response to this bald assertion, we asked why he thought that the market would tolerate such a high percentage of valueless activity. His explanation for why the 85 percent still seem to have jobs was as follows:

> So, there is friendship. There is investment banking still. Hey, you did this deal, I want you to cover me. There's a lot less than there used to be but dinners, games, free lunches, nice guy, he's got a family. There's all that shit that I think keeps people around. Sometimes I might be a benefit of it. Why do I have my job? Because I'm nice? I don't know. There's a lot of that too. I think it's not even corruption. It's just reality. We hire people that we like—*a lot*.

George thought through in detail his statement that 85 percent of analysts offered little to no value, and it is worth deconstructing in detail. First, as the mainstream research on sell-side analysts rightly points out, there are the conflicts of interest generated by a gamut of different investment banking opportunities. Specifically in this case, buy-side actors want their firms to have access to all upcoming initial public offerings (IPOs) and therefore will maintain relationships with sell-side analysts at a firm even if they find that these analysts offer few or no insights. They do so in the hope that these sell-side analysts will place them higher up on the list of those wishing to make initial investments. Second, there is the reciprocity and social cement generated by gifts and entertainment. However, another implication is that the accumulating interdependence between the buy-side and the sell-side, supported by deepening social ties, is a cause of inferior market analysis. Sell-side analysts keep their jobs and continue to have buy-side firms as their clients partly because of their ties and regardless of the quality or relevance of their research.

George's quote is also indicative of another inertia-supporting phenomenon—"cultural matching"[10]—whereby people who seem to fit in culturally are hired, a situation that tends to reproduce existing structures and behaviors. For example, it is revealing that George used the masculine "he" to describe a hypothetical sell-side analyst. If interviewees in our highly gendered sample—one, we should stress, that is still representative[11]— are all routinely engaged in hiring people that they like and get on with, this will likely tend toward the reproduction of a male-dominated field, with all the attendant social and cultural behaviors that go with it. Finally, George talked about the sympathy generated by simply being nice or having a family, which could explain his follow-up comment:

Yeah. There's guys that, still, why are we paying them $300,000? And they're like, we just cut them from $600,000 so you can't cut them to zero. It's like, whatever.

There is ambivalence in George's explanation of this phenomenon, which highlights the complex social structure of the field. On one hand, he lamented the persistence of well-paid and (what he sees as) underperforming analysts. On the other hand, he recognized the importance of social ties to the maintenance and reproduction of the field. He was genuinely conflicted by the economic drive for greater utility and the social imperative to maintain social cohesion. The field, as we learn from the findings, is populated not by purely economic (undersocialized) or purely social (oversocialized) actors but by reflective actors who understand and take into account various pressures and realities.

Similar views about the relation between the social structure of the field and the quality of analysis that the sell-side provides were expressed by other buy-side actors. For example, Derek, a buy-side analyst in Chicago with several years of experience, compared the value of sell-side analysts to that of expert networks. Expert networks are groups that bring together industry specialists who might be able to explain the implications of, say, a new regulation or patent for the prospects of a particular company or of an industry more broadly. Whereas fund managers might use sell-side analysts to broker meetings with company senior management in addition to offering company-specific analysis, expert networks such as Gerson Lehrman Group tend to glean insights from a variety of sources in the corporate/industry ecosystem in order to offer expert advice.[12] Derek rued the reality that the sell-side analysts who were part of the social structure in which he was also situated were paid multiples of what was paid to expert networks for what, in his view, often amounted to lower-quality insights into companies or industries. His explanation for why this was the case again literally evoked the sticky nature of social ties:

> I think human behavior is pretty habitual and sticky. And particularly this—I think this arrangement, if it changes, it'll be a slower change over time.

Derek's perception of social stickiness included frustration. He saw a situation that lacked economic efficiency and that hindered the flow of better-quality analysis. However, his perception was that, even with widespread recognition of such inefficiencies, it would be difficult to change the situation because of the congealed nature of social relationships.

The impact of social ties between the sell-side and the buy-side on the ability to generate insightful information is also evident when Alice (London, sell-side) discussed of her relationships with company management. These relationships, we were told, would often color her view of the company's prospects:

> It takes a level of familiarity with the company. . . . Say I have been supporting a company for three years; I've been very chummy with them because I believed in the company, but suddenly [a] lot of things change. How likely am I really to be negative?

Alice highlighted the challenges of writing a negative evaluation of your friends. Having spent years cultivating trust and friendship ("chummy" certainly denotes some level of friendship, however casual), you would be unlikely, according to Alice, to then jeopardize that for the sake of boosting your reputation with buy-side clients. More generally, Alice's concerns speak to the tensions between the social nature of the way in which knowledge is generated and the quality of that information. Social ties with company management are vital for getting timely and detailed information from the company, but they also create an implicit normative demand to put a positive spin on things. This normative demand is starkly illustrated by Ethan's experience in this vignette.

VIGNETTE: NORMS IN THE FIELD AND IMPACT ON SELL-SIDE RESEARCH

The accretion and cementing of social ties are accompanied by the establishment of norms that erect very real barriers to sell-side analysts being bearish on any company with which they have good relationships. This helps explain the widespread perception that these sell-side analysts are serving as the mouthpieces of company management rather than holding these companies to account or ensuring transparency in any way.

In a frank conversation on this issue, Ethan (Chicago, sell-side) revealed that his firm had an unwritten policy of never committing to a "sell" recommendation: i.e., never advising clients to sell the stock of any of the companies they follow. When asked why this was the case, he explained:

> There's a couple things you could point to. As you proba-bly already know, the investment banking [aspect]. I don't think we've ever had a sell-[rated] company do a deal with us, and I believe we get judged on internal metrics and sells just as well as buys. So, it's easiest just to put it as a neutral and not [recommend] it.

Ethan then went on to explain that although there are no written rules in his firm mandating this situation (as it would likely run afoul of securities regulations), a sell rating would mean that the company in question would never commit to doing future investment banking work with them, such as rais-ing additional debt or equity from the buy-side, a process that is invariably brokered by investment banks, which employ the vast majority of sell-side analysts.

It is not only investment banking opportunities that would be compromised by issuing a sell rating on a company. The gen-eral social brokerage activities that the sell-side undertakes on a regular basis, such a non-deal road shows, would also be nega-tively affected. These road shows are a key part of a company's investor relations program, during which company management travel to the offices of key institutional investors to discuss and explain financial results, milestones, strategy, and future pros-pects. These are often organized by the sell-side, and any threat to the sell-side's ability to put company management in front of their buy-side clients would negatively impact their revenue.

Going into further detail, Ethan, an analyst with just a few years of experience, recounted a recent scenario where he wrote a research note on a particular company that, in one sentence, suggested its earnings were likely to be negatively impacted by

(*Continued on next page*)

(*Continued from previous page*)

regulatory changes in Europe. Before being published, this note was shared with the company in question, which is a common practice in the field. The company's CFO then contacted the senior analyst in Ethan's office, who then asked Ethan to delete the sentence in question before the note went public. Ethan explained to us that situations such as this occur about once a quarter, but in any case, his firm self-disciplines by effectively not recommending "sells" at all and by trying to cover only companies that they think have good prospects:

> You'd rather be promoting your positive names: firms that will do business with you and generate money and will get people trading with you and road shows and get you at conferences.

This last quote speaks to the reciprocal nature of social ties and their impact on lowering the quality of knowledge created by the sell-side. Knowing that companies prefer positive interpretations, sell-side companies tend to prefer better companies, leaving those with less certain prospects (where ironically their services would be needed more) with less coverage by the analyst community. Then, as Ethan's quotes show, negative comments are censored effectively through pressure from management. The strength of these norms is such that even in relatively extreme circumstances, such as covering a company that turns out not to be a positive name and that has actively been misleading investors, sell-side firms are reluctant to recommend a "sell." Ethan offered an example of a company his sell-side firm was covering that had distorted earnings figures for an acquisition it had undertaken in Europe by emphasizing what it called "synergistic EBITDA" rather than EBITDA.[13] In other words, the company was pushing what Ethan saw as a rather fanciful financial projection. Two weeks before earnings results were announced, it became clear that the company was not going to make its earnings target, and, indeed, Ethan was extremely bearish on its prospects going forward:

> The first thing I said [to] the senior analyst I was with—I was like "This one's going to zero." And I think it's selling for like two dollars now, [when] it was upwards of twenty dollars at the time. You just know that these are bad management teams, no real operating process, tough end markets, or I guess flat end markets in their case. So, it was just a combination of three things.

However, despite this skepticism, Ethan's firm placed only a neutral rating on the stock in order to save face and to send a signal to the rest of the corporate world that the firm was still a sell-side firm that could be used for investment banking work:

> We were comanagers on a deal, on an equity offering actually a couple weeks prior to earnings release, and we left it as a neutral, although in hindsight that would have been the easiest sell, but in a case like that, we just put it to neutral and then moved on.

This example shows the deep social roots of the conflicts of interest that exist between sell-side firms and company management. The firms that sell-side analysts work for see the corporate world as their clients for a raft of investment banking work, so there is active pressure on their research divisions to not upset the apple cart. This is confirmed by the observation in the academic literature that objective research analysis, which is paid for by buy-side clients, is compromised by the desire to curry favor with company management, who might also employ the sell-side firm to broker an equity offering or some other investment banking opportunity.

(Continued on next page)

(*Continued from previous page*)

Our analysis adds an important element to this observation. The dynamics between the sell-side and company management, which result in biased interpretation being communicated to investors, are facilitated by the social structure of the field of investment advice. In some respects, the real client of the sell-side is company management rather than the buy-side, a phenomenon that has been hinted at by prior research.[14] In particular, the readiness of sell-side firms to twist their reports is based on long-established norms that define, implicitly but clearly enough, the expectations of the sell-side in the quid-pro-quo described here. The transactional part of the interaction is only the tip of the iceberg. The submerged part is the understanding of everyone's role, including the necessary informal nature of the market itself. In addition, this shows us that actors on the buy-side are well aware of this set of normative demands and accept it because they want to maintain an infrastructure of relations that is overall still useful to them, as we will explore in the following section.

BROKER STICKINESS: BUNDLING

Networks of interpersonal relationships often have to confront or serve as an infrastructure for broader sets of interorganizational relationships and interests.[15] Our findings include the repeated characterization—from both buy-side and sell-side interviewees—of sell-side analysts as a kind of add-on, wrap-around sweetener offered by investment banks to clients as part of a wider bundle of services. In this respect, sell-side analysts are seen as being in the marketplace not solely to provide advice, even if that is their ostensible role but also to generate corporate finance work for their investment bank. In fact, the existence of interorganizational connections, where the economic influence of interests is much more pronounced than in the case of interpersonal connections, emphasizes further the impact that the social structure of field has on the quality of information produced. This point, colorfully expressed by Ethan earlier, was reinforced by several other sell-side analysts:

> I know of some analysts—I won't mention names—but I know of some analysts especially within my sector where they're there to get banking business. . . . I'm sure others hold this opinion as well, but it's very obvious. When they get on a conference call [with company management], they're not as tuned in as somebody else [analysts at firms without investment banking relationships]. (Shaun, New York)

> The fact is, I think, their revenue is pretty much entirely driven by banking business. I think the fact is, today, that [this] pretty much describes the business model of pretty much everyone on the sell side. (Eric, New York)

These sell-side analysts were therefore extremely clear that their paychecks were effectively written by the companies about which they were supposed to be writing critical assessments. As we noted previously, the buy-side is also well aware of this and often is quite dismissive of the value of research produced by the sell-side. Yet even if the research provided by the sell-side analyst is not valued, the sell-side will continue to produce it, and the buy-side will continue to pay for it because that sell-side analysis acts as a portal to other investment banking services that buy-side actors need to access:

> Maybe you [as a buy-side analyst] don't need the research from that [sell-side] analyst, but you're never going to turn off [the sell-side firm] because you use them for all of the other services that they provide. (Drew, New York, sell-side)

In fact, several interviewees stressed that it is only the reliance on investment banks that justified paying commissions to certain sell-side firms. For example, when pressed about why his former buy-side firm kept paying commissions to sell-side analysts, Ivan, now on the sell-side in New York, responded: "I mean, like I'm not going to bullshit you. It's corporate finance," referring to access to the stocks of IPOs being managed by the sell-side firm. Although these kinds of incentives have been targeted by regulations such as MiFID II in Europe, which specifically requires investment banks to charge clients separately for research and corporate finance/investment banking work,[16] interviewees pointed out that this had succeeded only in moving firms from "a direct compensation structure to an indirect compensation structure" (Amal, Chicago, buy-side) and that the conflicts of interest generated by myriad investment banking services still existed: "Nobody says it out loud, [but] no doubt that it's there."

Many sell-side actors were conscious that their commissions were more dependent on what their brokerage firms did than on the quality of their research. Again, this open secret is tolerated and, indeed, actively sustained by the buy-side because of wider interorganizational dependencies that exist in the field, as attested to by Drew, a buy-side actor from New York:

And maybe I characterized their [the buy-side] view generally of research as a little pessimistic. They still like the service, but right, they have to cut costs somewhere, and so they'll look around the landscape, and they'll say, "Okay, who do I not need research from?" And candidly maybe you don't need the research from that JPMorgan analyst, but you're never going to turn off JPMorgan because you use them for all of the other services that they provide.

The preeminence of brokerage capacity (referring to the actual trading of shares, for which the buy-side also uses investment banks) over research insights was emphasized by Nico, an experienced sell-side analyst from New York, who lamented the ways in which his firm's limited brokerage capacity often meant that his research insights seemed to be offered to clients for free:

I may talk to a client and pitch him on a stock, right? And the client may say, "This is great idea. We're going to buy the stock." Unfortunately, we may not be trading or trafficking in that stock. So he may call Morgan Stanley, for example, and say, "We want to buy a million shares." Again, use the example of Coca-Cola, right? So they may buy Coca-Cola through Morgan Stanley because Morgan Stanley has a million shares to sell at this point, right?

Nico highlighted the importance of belonging to a firm that has broad coverage and deep trading volume so that his research would ultimately be paid for indirectly by trading commissions. Without the wider brokerage functions, Nico felt that his research was a free resource for which he didn't get sufficient credit. Thus, while many sell-side analysts lamented the fact that the quality of their research was often compromised by brokerage and investment banking opportunities, they still clung to this state of affairs because they and their firms were at least be rewarded via these mechanisms, albeit indirectly.

Relatedly other interviewees from the buy-side commented that trading commissions paid to the top five investment banks cover the costs of their analysts, with little need to generate revenue from research, allowing these firms to hire relatively inexperienced analysts:

> That's why [an investment bank] hires twenty-six-year-olds and pays them two hundred grand, because . . . they're still going to get plenty of trading commissions. (Alan, Chicago, buy-side)

Although a $200,000 annual salary might appear quite generous, especially for an analyst only a couple of years out of college, the implication of Alan's comment is that this level is relatively low for the field. Additionally, he suggested that the investment bank had little incentive to hire experienced analysts (at significantly higher salaries) who produced higher-quality research because it may not lead to an incremental level of revenue that would cover the higher cost of analysts' compensation.

Conversely, while the bundling of services can explain why younger, inexperienced analysts are preferred over those who could potentially produce more informed research, it also explains why some older, more experienced analysts persist in the field even when they are viewed as long past their prime. Some sell-side analysts are perceived as being around in the market simply because they have always been there. That is, either they or the brokerage house to which they are attached has historically been used to execute trades for certain buy-side clients, so the analyst continues to get paid. This is illustrated for us by Louis, a fund manager from Chicago:

> I don't know, but clearly the market's thin, and you know it's pretty typical, for example, and . . . by the way, the guy who does our trading, he's been there forever. You know he's been there since 1985, 1986. So, he's got these relationships with these guys all over the place. Okay, and so he might have a guy who's a broker for somebody, and works as a broker, actually managing individuals' accounts. But that person's been in place for so long for that particular geography and has such a well-developed set of clients that, I mean, he ends up starting to be a conduit for volume.

Being a "conduit for volume" refers to the phenomenon when an analyst, whose ostensible job is to offer research insights, becomes a de facto gatekeeper for brokerage activities for a particular set of clients or industry sector. In other words, the analyst works for a firm that has access to a lot of buyers and sellers of stocks, so they can execute trades with ease.

Louis didn't necessarily lament this situation, although he did allude wryly to the peculiarities of paying someone who is of limited or no use in terms of research. Indeed, he suggested that if there is a broker "out there who can bring us that flow, it is a good thing." Buy-side actors are not interested solely in research insights. Even when faced with a sell-side analyst who is trying to push ideas, they will look beyond this to the other activities and services that the sell-side analyst's firm may be able to offer them.

Because sell-side analysts are motivated to promote stocks, generate commissions, and get capital inflows, many buy-side actors conclude that these analysts are not really incentivized to produce high-quality interpretations and accurate forecasts. Even if their research is of poor quality, they can still be handsomely compensated because their employer is engaged in a lot of brokerage and corporate finance work. As Jae, a sell-side analyst in New York, bluntly pointed out: "They could be wrong and make a ton of money."

Although we know the buy-side does not value the sell-side for its ability to forecast stock price fluctuations, it is not clear whether this is because the sell-side has never have been good at this or because the buy-side simply accepts the sell-side's conflicts of interests as a fact of life. What is clear, however, is that the quality of research has diminished further in recent years. The incentives on the sell-side to generate trading volume ahead of research insights has led to a bias toward more short-term analysis. Several of our interviewees noted the increasing dominance of short-term investors, especially hedge funds, in the sell-side business model and the concomitant impact of this on research output, which they saw as becoming much more short-term in orientation and less interpretative.

There was a sense among some more experienced buy-side actors that the sell-side had been slowly losing its value and centrality to the buy-side's investment decision-making process. Over time, sell-side analysts have become more incentivized by investment banking business, but they are still perceived by many in the field as there to offer investment advice. In this respect, perceptions might lag reality, which indicates a level of cognitive inertia, something that has been noted as prevalent in other economic fields as well.[17] In turn, those perceptions are actively maintained in part by sell-side analysts themselves, who continued to project an image of trusted consiglieri via the regular publication of research reports and earnings revisions.

BROKER STICKINESS: INTERNAL DIVISIONS ON THE BUY-SIDE

Dynamics around the bundling of services offer plausible explanations for why some financial analysts persist in the marketplace even though they are not always valued for their research insights. More mundane forms of broker stickiness also exist and were alluded to by the more junior members of buy-side teams we interviewed. For example, take the following statement from Dylan, the junior buy-side analyst from Chicago who had been in the field for less than two years: "So getting in touch [with a particular sell-side analyst] is also driven by the economics of who we actually pay."

This quote is interesting because this junior analyst would have more interaction with the sell-side than his boss (the portfolio manager), who was somewhat removed from the nuts and bolts of research insights on individual stocks. Yet from the point of view of those who were consuming the sell-side research (i.e., the junior buy-side analysts), they simply use the research for which they already have a subscription. Rather than identifying the best analysts and then paying for their research, the buy-side uses the analysts they are already paying. One might expect that portfolio managers have previously identified the best analysts, but given that these managers are somewhat removed from observing the performance of sell-side analysts on a day-to-day basis, it is reasonable to presume that their roster of sell-side analysts might not reflect those who offer the best research insights.

This notion of getting what you have already paid for rather than paying for what you need is evident in the following exchange, which was prompted when Jingqi, a buy-side analyst in Chicago, stated that her firm had access to about ten analysts who were following companies in her particular industry sectors:

> INTERVIEWER: If there are thirty people out here, or twenty-five, that do this [sell-side analysis] for a living, you're a large client, you're interested in the space. Why are you not using the other twenty?
>
> JINGQI: First and foremost, we don't have access to everyone.

One might have expected the respondent to say something along the lines of "We think that the ten we use are more helpful" or to offer some other utilitarian explanation, but in this instance, the reason was more primordial and less conscious than that. The explanation offered by both Dylan and Jingqi centers on the research that happens to be available to them. Again, it may be that this analyst's superiors had identified the best sell-side analysts and entered into arrangements with them, but Jingqi, who was actually consuming that research, did not say this, and neither did Dylan.

The key implication of these exchanges is that many buy-side actors tend to privilege existing relationships. Indeed, the stickiness metaphor cropped up again when Reuben, a buy-side analyst from Chicago, was describing relationships in the field. Although on the buy-side when we spoke with him, he had previously worked for several years as a sell-side analyst so he was well-placed to comment on the nature of these relationships. Having two vantage points enabled him to observe how relationships might develop or congeal over time:

> I think, at [my buy-side firm] at least—and I think this is similar across the buy-side shops—there's a very strong stickiness with your existing brokers [sell-side analysts' firms]. You don't want to develop new relationships. And the most sticky ones are the big guys. It's the Citi, the Wells, the Goldman Sachs.

The reluctance to develop new relationships here is suggestive of a bandwidth or effort issue, where it is recognized that new relationships entail additional, discretionary work. This may explain, at least in part, why the sell-side analysts with the most accurate financial forecasts and price targets do not automatically jump to the top of the investor polls: the buy-side is slow to move on from an existing sell-side relationship, and there is not enough bandwidth or budget to have unlimited relationships. Reuben went further, explaining how changing the roster of "go-to" analysts for a particular buy-side firm was a real challenge because of the bonds between his superiors (Todd and Matt) and their sell-side contacts:

> So, I think Todd and Matt really drive it: these eight or nine analysts. It is very hard to get that to change, which I found . . . because I come in and I say, "Hey. Some things that [sell-side firm] does, from my experience, [are] actually pretty valuable. I think it would benefit me if I were to read that." Or I'm like "Hey. These analysts know what they're talking about. I would value their opinion." But it's really interesting to see that for them to change off that tiered structure—that nine, if you will—they're very sticky, right. We're not changing in rank. And we're not really changing who's on there and who's not.

It may well be that Todd and Matt had a different sense of what is valuable than Reuben did, but the implication is that the "tiered structure" that was in place in terms of which analysts were worth speaking to is a function of legacy relationships, the bundling of services, and historical factors rather than a strict, up-to-date assessment of who is actually most valuable in terms of research insights.

CONCLUSION

We have seen from the interactions between sell-side and buy-side actors that a number of social factors are of paramount importance in structuring the investment field. On one level, and confirming suspicions that are foundational to sociology,[18] habit and routine are clearly evident in the practices of both sets of actors. Moreover, these habits and routines are supported and bolstered by various forms of interpersonal and interorganizational dependencies. A key theme to emerge is that human behavior and human relationships are sticky and changing practices or disrupting these relationships is difficult, or even unthinkable, for many, even if more economically efficient and rational ways of doing things are hypothetically possible.

Beyond this stickiness, we have seen that the field is riddled with, but not riven by, conflicts of interest. Conflicts of interest abound as those on the sell-side, who are positioned between investors and their investment objects, try hard to keep both happy and operate effectively as a necessary conduit that connects the two. Yet the field is not riven by these conflicts of interest, as the various parties appear to be aware of them and tolerate them for diverse reasons. For example, the buy-side is well aware that the sell-side analysts' research is compromised by their need to curry favor with company management. This does bother those on the buy-side and prompts them to castigate sell-side analysts as the "mouthpieces of management" (Murray, Chicago, buy-side), but buy-side actors know that they can get the research insights they need from expert networks and use the sell-side for concierge services like non-deal road shows, general brokerage activities, and access to future capital-raising rounds.[19] Indeed, in some ways the buy-side not only tolerates these conflicts of interest but also actively benefits from them: tapping into the congealed infrastructure of relations with the sell-side at the center gives the buy-side privileged access to IPOs and seasoned equity offerings.

Overall, a cocktail of habit, routine, social sensibilities, convenience, and self-interest shapes the structure of the field of investment advice. While these various factors appear to be mutually reinforcing, they do directly counteract each other at times. They nevertheless exist in some sort of balance/creative tension that provides stability and permits field participants to act in purposeful ways that maintain or advance their own field positions.[20] The rules of the game in the field of investment advice are complex and contradictory, but they are not completely opaque to field members.

Chapter Four

CONFORMITY AND CONSENSUS

Excellence in most societies means playing in accordance with the rules of the game.
　　　　—Pierre Bourdieu, "La Fabrique des Débats Publics"

THE INVESTMENT field is amenable to social and institutional pressure in ways besides the persistent, sticky social ties, habits, and routines illustrated in chapter 3. This is evident from the way in which analysts participate in the production of consensus numbers, an omnipresent feature of the investment world. Regularly updated on market data platforms such as Bloomberg, they constitute the aggregate opinion of equity analysts vis-à-vis a particular stock, bond, or commodity.[1] To win plaudits from the buy-side, the sell-side is pressured to diverge from consensus opinion and produce investment advice that is truly differentiated. However, our research reveals that being bold in this fashion is risky: being out of consensus is fine when you are right, but if you are wrong, you will likely suffer a credibility challenge as an analyst. As a result, the majority of analysts tend to converge around consensus numbers in order to play it safe. This phenomenon is exacerbated by the reality of needing to curry favor with company management (discussed in chapter 3), which often guides analysts toward estimates and opinions that their companies are able to beat.[2] We find that these social ties with management, combined with risk-averse attitudes, push analysts toward a herd mentality and tend to discourage innovation and boldness, albeit with some exceptions.

Once again, economic approaches struggle to explain why this situation has transpired. Instead, the social dynamics of fields—specifically the anxiety actors feel due to the pressure to maintain field position[3] and avoid the penalties that arise from making inaccurate predictions—offer better explanations for why financial intermediaries behave the way they do. Taken together, the findings in chapter 3 on social stickiness and in this chapter evidence widespread inertia and stability in the field of investment advice. As interpersonal and inter-institutional relationships congeal over time, a dense social network forms that allows many actors to maintain field position. However, paradoxically perhaps, the information signals emitted from this dense social network to the wider market take a relatively shallow and narrow form because status is not conferred on the basis of deep narrative exchange, as might be expected in the case of a dense social network. Rather, the social nature of evaluation in the field prompts the majority of field actors to revert to an intellectual mean rather than acting on conviction. Overall, this leads to the view that the field is at once socially inert and intellectually conservative.

CONSENSUS AS A CENTRIPETAL FORCE

Consensus numbers for a particular stock are generally the aggregated earnings forecasts of all analysts covering that stock for a given quarter or financial year.[4] They are published on platforms such as Bloomberg, Visible Alpha, and Morningstar.com and by other widely used informational outlets. The most dominant of these is Bloomberg, which boasts about 365,000 terminals on the desks of investment bankers, bond traders, equity analysts, pension fund managers, sovereign wealth fund managers, and central bank officials. Every day these terminals process an average of more than 300 billion bits of financial information and send about 1.4 billion messages and 30 million "Instant Bloomberg" chat messages that ricochet around the world.[5] They are a ubiquitous feature of financial markets and have been for several decades. Because of this, we decided to explore practices related to consensus numbers for the purposes of this book. If all actors in the field are paying attention to consensus numbers in some way, then they represent an opportune prism through which to obtain insight into the social dynamics of the field.

VIGNETTE: THE CONSENSUS CRUTCH

Our interviewees confirmed the omnipresence of consensus numbers in the field, describing them as a crucial part of the calculative process by which actors on both the buy-side and the sell-side arrive at their respective valuations of company stock.

(*Continued on next page*)

(*Continued from previous page*)

For example, take the following explanation from Kevin, a mid-career buy-side analyst in Chicago:

> We do our own internal cash flow modeling for our companies. And we'll [ask]: "Hey, are there big deviations between what we're forecasting versus what the market is perceiving to be achievable?" And the only way to put a gauge on what the market feels is to look at consensus numbers, right?

As this quote indicates, consensus numbers serve as benchmarks for assessing the validity of a particular valuation. In fact, consensus numbers had become a taken-for-granted element of Kevin's calculative process. Our interviewees repeatedly referred to consensus numbers as representing the "aggregate opinion" of the market vis-à-vis asset prices. Importantly, as a result of this perception of consensus numbers as indicative of the market, they have come to play a central role in many calculative practices. This is curious because buy-side actors were, in the main, uninterested in the forecasts or price targets put out by individual analysts. However, when these individual forecasts were aggregated, they took on a different significance for the buy-side. Again, the views of Kevin on this point are instructive:

> What if the sell-side didn't exist? You then wouldn't have these numbers out there to anchor on, that we pay so much attention to. . . . Then we, on the buy-side, . . . wouldn't have a crutch, if you will, from the sell-side analysts.

Kevin's use of the crutch metaphor suggests not only that consensus numbers are helpful but also that they are necessary—that without them the buy-side's efficient operation would be hindered. Our interview material reveals that this dependency on consensus numbers is both multifaceted and deep-rooted. For example, because of their inclusion at early stages in the calculative process, consensus numbers were incorporated into the arguments being developed and then communicated by buy-side or sell-side actors without necessarily being scrutinized directly for their validity:

> I think a lot of people on the buy-side will have a sector evaluation sheet or [will be asking] "What's consensus estimates?" . . . "What's the price?"—and then therefore "What's the multiple?" (Kevin, Chicago, buy-side)

As this quote indicates, consensus numbers are fed into buy-side decision-making as supporting evidence for opinions. This increases the importance of consensus numbers in stealth-like fashion: the reliance on the consensus numbers is hidden within the calculation that supports an argument. That is, for one to criticize the reliability of the argument, they may need to deconstruct it, as by now the consensus numbers serve as an infrastructure for developing opinions rather than as visible building blocks in the calculative process. Otherwise put, consensus numbers are both visible and invisible at the same time: they become embedded as ubiquitous, taken-for-granted facts of life in financial markets, but because they are embedded, it is not always obvious to all participants how they have influenced individual opinions or estimates. Indeed, the reality that many individual opinions anchor on consensus initially leads to a certain recursiveness in opinion forming in the field more generally.

Although buy-side actors frequently questioned how individual sell-side analysts arrived at their individual forecasts, they

(*Continued on next page*)

(*Continued from previous page*)

tended to question the validity of the aggregate consensus numbers less often. This differential treatment of predictions can be explained by the fact that consensus numbers are not associated with any specific actor. This, perhaps paradoxically, lends consensus numbers a protected status of sorts. That is, although these numbers are based on calculations from the sell-side, they are compiled and published by a seemingly disinterested party (e.g., Bloomberg) and thus are regarded as a de facto standard when assessing the market.

The privileged status granted to consensus numbers, however, does not prevent market participants such as Kevin from attempting to "clean them up" by applying statistical logic:

> You kind of can break that out [Bloomberg consensus numbers] between the twenty sell-side names that are up there . . . and maybe there are a couple of outliers. It's pretty obvious that [with] those outliers, there's something wrong in their numbers. . . . So, if you have some [real] strugglers that are on the low side or high side, . . . you cut those three names out.

Aiming to reduce the complexity of the informational signal he received, Kevin treated the different predictions as if they belonged to a normal distribution, in which the observations that appear more frequently are more trusted. The outliers are presumed to be wrong for various reasons. This quick statistical cleanup provided Kevin with the comfort of having what he perceived as more robust numbers. Equally, this practice had the unintended consequence of amplifying the impact of the average consensus number and the individual opinions associated with it.

CONSENSUS NUMBERS AS SAFE

Based on the foregoing, consensus is seen as very important by actors in the field; actor-network theorists might refer to it as a kind of "obligatory passage point."[6] Moreover, the practices that these actors undertake (such as deconstructing the consensus along normal distribution parameters) serve to further enshrine the consensus as a ubiquitous anchor in financial markets. This causes many on both the sell-side and the buy-side to be nervous about departing from consensus:

> You need to be within 5 or 10 percent of consensus. . . . You don't want to be that analyst who's got your head way above the parapet, . . . you've only got so many bullets that you can [use to] make these bold calls, and you made . . . one last year and it didn't work out. So you're like, fuck, I'm not going to do that again, I'm going to stay inside consensus. (Terence, London, buy-side)

In this quote, which is indicative of a more generalized view, Terence framed consensus numbers as a possible shelter from mistakes. A sell-side analyst expressed this view more succinctly: "If you're with consensus and you're wrong, it's fine because you're with consensus" (Salim, London, sell-side). In general, these two quotes show how the pressure analysts feel to avoid erroneous predictions is operationalized through consensus numbers, since these are used ultimately by the market to measure errors or accuracy.

These ongoing pressures to align with consensus numbers are identifiable from a wide array of practices in our interview data. One's own judgment and professionalism or those of other actors are scrutinized using consensus numbers as a benchmark and as a basis for interrogation. For example, the extent to which the results of a particular analyst's model align with consensus numbers is regarded as a proxy for the quality of the analyst. Alan, an experienced buy-side actor in Chicago, expressed this view as he described the way in which he attempted to coach his stable of sell-side analysts into being closer to consensus: "I used to go pick up people's [sell-side] models and tell them where they were wrong when they were too far off consensus."

The belief that compliance with consensus numbers is indicative of high-quality predictions is reflected even more frequently in our interviews with both buy-side and sell-side actors, who stated that they commonly questioned their own predictions when their calculations diverged from consensus numbers. This is true even for seasoned fund managers:

> You know just kind of checking because I thought that I was below consensus meaningfully. . . . So [I'm] like "Damn, what am I, are you seeing something here because you know, . . . is there a fundamental operating issue that's driving that that I'm missing?" (Louis, Chicago, buy-side)

Louis's quote suggests how deep-rooted consensus-related practices are in the field. Consensus numbers signal to the actor how they stand in relation to the aggregate view of their peer group, thereby helping them to develop a "feel for the game."[7]

This profound internalization of a numerical figure and its acceptance as a performance indicator show that consensus plays an important role in the structure of the field. Acting in relation to consensus numbers is taken for granted and becomes part of the habitus of investment professionals.

The self-discipline that many actors exhibit when aligning with consensus numbers suggests that consensus alignment is an unwritten rule of the game in the field of investment advice. Indeed, whenever actors do not act in accordance with this particular rule, there appear to be negative consequences for them. If actors try to diverge from consensus, they will most likely find themselves facing social pressure from other field participants to fall back in line with it. This social pressure is well expressed by Terence (London, buy-side), who rolled his eyes as he described the tiresome process of having to justify to people why he might be out of consensus:

> Then there's the really annoying conversations that we have with people, and they'll be like "You are 5 percent blah, blah, blah, above consensus in three years."

Here Terence was criticizing the type of argument he heard frequently from investors who challenged his views on the basis of divergence from consensus numbers. He expressed his frustration with the oversimplification that consensus-led discourse is perceived to impose, much in the same way that a physician might be annoyed at patients who turn up at a clinic after having googled a list of medical symptoms. We noticed repeatedly how actors felt constrained by the omnipresence of consensus numbers and the widespread belief in them, even though their own practices reproduced this social pressure to align with consensus numbers. In this respect, they railed against a social norm that they themselves had constructed and given life to by continually acting in accordance with it.

One of the common reactions to this social pressure was to explicitly try to ignore consensus numbers, at least when preparing predictions. We often heard that actors, although aware of the constitutive effects of consensus, tried to avoid looking at consensus numbers until after they had established their view. Terence (London, buy-side) even said that he "will not look at the consensus for that number at all until I've done all that modeling." This is much like a teenager studying for an exam by answering textbook sample questions while trying to avoid looking at the solution pages at the end of the book. The reality though is that investment professionals are always taking a sneak peek at consensus. Indeed, as illustrated here, it is hard to avoid consensus numbers even when an actor doesn't fully believe in them—such is the seriousness with which they are taken by the field generally. In this regard, consensus serves as a centripetal force. Those who attempt to diverge from it find themselves caught up in its spin cycle and end up failing to escape its pull.

CONSENSUS AS A CENTRIFUGAL FORCE

The previous section illustrated the norms, perceptions, and social pressures that pull buy-side and sell-side actors toward consensus numbers, treating these as both a fact of life and a safe space. Equally, in a world that putatively rewards alpha generation[8] and distinctiveness[9] as part of an overarching attempt to "beat the market," there are simultaneous pressures pushing actors away from consensus figures, which we discuss in this section.

DIVERGENCE FROM CONSENSUS
AS A SIGNAL OF EXCELLENCE

While some see consensus figures as representative of the average intelligent opinion in the marketplace, others such as Ethan, a sell-side analysis in Chicago, see them more disparagingly— as reflecting a hypothetical average investor:

> When I think about the average investor, I think about somebody who knows the story, who probably hasn't looked at it since the earnings call, and somebody who would probably need, I don't know, fifteen, twenty minutes to get up to speed on the name. So I think of an average investor as the consensus.

Ambitious sell-side and buy-side actors wish to distinguish themselves from such run-of-the-mill investors. As such, this self-styled investment elite tend to see consensus numbers less as a safe haven and more as a starting point in a process of devising a differentiated opinion about market prices. In this respect, they find it important to pay attention to consensus in order to distance themselves from it. Such a view was expressed by Pierce, an experienced sell-side analyst from Chicago. We noticed that he was, like many of our other interviewees, talking about consensus as if it was a fact of life, so we probed him on why he would pay so much attention to it:

> INTERVIEWER: Why do you care about the consensus?
> PIERCE: I think you need to know why you're different.

There are two key points in this quote: first, the need to be different from consensus in the first place was important to Pierce; and, second, anticipating that other market actors would inevitably ask why his predictions diverged from consensus, Pierce needed to think carefully about why they did. He went on to point out that explaining the rationale behind your divergence from consensus was a good way to communicate with potential buy-side clients:

> I think understanding why [consensus numbers are] too high and what risk that poses in the near term can still be important. Then you can communicate that to clients: "Hey, I think Moody's estimates need to come down because I think people are still too high on their leverage loads and structured finance estimates."

By carefully deconstructing consensus numbers and explaining to buy-side actors why and how they are wrong, sell-side analysts have the opportunity to demonstrate their own expertise and capture more of the mind share of the clients that they so covet.

Diverging from consensus is risky, but for those who felt confident enough to do so, they saw their divergence as a way to signal excellence to the buy-side:

I've been trying not to look at [consensus numbers] . . . why does anyone on the buy-side want to read something that a young analyst has just copied from the Street? Shouldn't I be the one setting the numbers? Shouldn't I be the one thinking about what the growth rates are? (Ethan, Chicago, sell-side)

Here "the Street" here refers to Wall Street, even though Ethan was in Chicago, and is a shorthand for the market in general. He extolled the virtues of the ostensible role of the sell-side analyst, outlining the importance of in-depth research that produces a differentiated opinion.[10] In sociological terms, this is the reification of a desired ideal type.[11] It is noteworthy that this was a young analyst who still believed ostensible, official rationale for the existence of equity research analysts. There was something charmingly naive about his attachment to the explicit rules of the game, although it was simultaneously cruel because he had yet to learn that the explicit and tacit rules of the game contradict one another. For the time being, he was emotionally invested in the illusio of the sell-side analyst. The field causes actors to want to be like this ideal type, but generally most do not dare; because they are cognizant of the risks involved in trying to produce differentiated opinions, they instead play it safe by going along with the rest of the Street. An older, more experienced respondent may well have framed the main role of equity analysts in terms of trading volume, CEO babysitting, and the safeguarding of future investment banking opportunities.

Nevertheless, other sell-side analysts also saw themselves as pursuing differentiated opinions that, according to them, could end up generating alpha for their buy-side clients. Salim

(London) said, "Over a long time I think a better analyst who has different ideas from consensus can generate alpha." Agreeing with him about differentiation was Nico (New York): "A fresh well-thought-out estimate is the most important thing, especially if it ends up being out of consensus."

These quotes reflect the belief, held by some but not all, that a core competency of analysts on both the sell-side and the buy-side is the ability to develop an interpretation of market conditions that differs from the prevalent view on the Street or in "the City" (London). Not only was this a view held by some on the sell-side, but also actors on the buy-side were actively seeking to produce differentiated insights that could drive alpha-generating investment decisions. Reuben, a Chicago buy-side analyst reporting to a fund manager, clearly expressed this:

> So, a big value-add that I can give to [my boss] is saying that "this is what [the] consensus number is. I think that there's no way they're going to hit this. Consensus estimates have to come down on this name." Then I think that really does drive our investment decisions.

Overall, although the majority of our respondents evinced a desire to stay within consensus, a significant number sought to actively distance themselves from consensus. Whether these latter individuals were successful in doing so is beyond the scope of the present work, but overwhelming evidence suggests that they would be unlikely to do so on anything like a consistent basis. This notwithstanding, for the purposes of this study we view these arguments about seeking to diverge from consensus as interesting for a number of reasons. First, these individuals drew distinctions between themselves as more elite players in the field and others whom they characterized as "average," thereby showing how the field follows an agonistic logic.[12] The investment field is divided and contains multiple subgroups or communities that have different dispositions and endowments of capital.[13] Second, that they were striving for distinctiveness shows again that many had bought into the illusio of the trusted investment consigliere even though buy-side actors were relatively blunt about sell-side analysts being valuable to them mostly because of the concierge and brokerage services they offered.[14] Third, that they were striving for distinctiveness in an environment that values conformity means this group of self-styled elite consensus breakers is the exception that proves the rule: excellence often means conforming to social pressures or acting in accordance with the rules of the game.[15]

CRITICISMS OF CONSENSUS NUMBERS

The foregoing suggests a complicated set of practices and behaviors vis-à-vis consensus numbers in the investment field. In one respect, consensus numbers are a ubiquitous anchor point, and in another, they are a point of departure that some analysts will diverge from only with trepidation. It is important here to make a distinction between the social nature of consensus numbers and their epistemic virtues—between the *realpolitik* of consensus and its scientific validity. We have already discussed the former, but it is worthwhile for us to spend some time exploring the latter because doing so throws the dynamics of the field into further relief.

One key criticism of consensus numbers, emanating from the buy-side, is that sell-side analysts don't update their earnings forecasts (the raw ingredients of consensus numbers) on a timely enough basis. Reuben, who had worked on the sell-side before moving to a buy-side analyst position in Chicago, explained that this situation arose through what he saw as a combination of laziness and limited manpower:

> Usually, every analyst is at least updating between quarters from their earnings releases. But let's say between quarters, if there was a material impact that changed, some analysts won't update their numbers until they're like "Well, I'll just wait until earnings season." Then the consensus number up there is really kind of skewed because let's say half the analysts have updated, half haven't. . . . They just don't have the resources. Your sell-side analyst maybe is covering like fifty names or something and doesn't have a team. Maybe it's just one guy or something.

Reuben lamented the quality of the overall aggregate figure but did imply that there were some good analysts out there who produced timely, more robust estimates. Similar views were expressed by other buy-side actors, such as Alan (Chicago), who had spent a lot of time coaching sell-side analysts and pointing out when they had made mistakes. He described a situation where he found that a sell-side analyst's earnings forecast contained a basic mathematical error:

You know, you'd be like whatever, 20 percent off consensus and you didn't realize it was because you had an Excel error. It's like "Oh my God, and you upgraded the stock on it." Right? I'm like "How do you get to these earnings? It makes no sense." And I asked for the model and go through it. I'm like "Oh my God, you made a math error." Right? And lots of times people would not want to correct it.

Alan expressed frustration here at what he saw as a relatively common situation on the sell-side. The quote is interesting for a number of reasons. First, it demonstrates again that consensus is the benchmark against which individual forecasts are judged; second, it shows how individual forecasts that make up consensus contain errors; and third, it points toward a social dynamic in which analysts do not want to correct their mistakes because they are embarrassed and would prefer to save face.

Both Reuben and Alan cast aspersions on the veracity or usefulness of consensus numbers. Their arguments also imply a field that is highly varied and heterogeneous, populated by those who are better resourced and focused and those who are struggling to offer sufficient coverage or accurate analysis for various reasons. In conceptual terms, this suggests a division between the dominant and the dominated,[16] but because we are relying on the narratives of individuals with skin in the game, we should obviously treat such characterizations with circumspection. There is a tendency in the money management business for actors to see themselves as the masters of the universe.[17]

It is tempting to suggest that any such heterogeneity in the field is closely coupled with quality or skill levels. In other words, we might conclude that consensus huggers offer more average performance, whereas those seeking to diverge from consensus are more closely associated with alpha generation. However, we do not have results that corroborate such a view. Rather, our results lead us to conclude that the relationship between financial intermediaries and consensus is multifaceted and context dependent. Those pursuing different investment strategies might have different needs in terms of anchoring on consensus. For example, we were told that generalists—i.e., those who didn't focus on a specific sector—tended to rely more on consensus numbers:

> If you think about generalist money in the space, I mean the guys that aren't really doing the detailed independent work. [It is these guys] that are relying on the sell side on consensus numbers to drive their valuation. (Kevin, Chicago, buy-side)

Those pursuing more generalist research strategies tend to have a larger investment universe, follow more stocks, and therefore have more need of the sell-side. By extension, generalists also tend to rely more on consensus numbers. Specialists, in contrast, tend to have a smaller universe of stocks to choose from, so they are able to be more up to speed on the companies within that investable universe and have less reason to lean on the sell-side to fill in any gaps in their knowledge.

Equally, there are temporal elements to the attention paid to consensus numbers. For example, Kevin (Chicago, buy-side) explained that consensus was more robust after a certain period of time: "I would say probably at [a] twelve-month period is where you feel a higher level of comfort on consensus numbers."

In this respect, consensus is not seen naively as the gospel truth from the outset; rather, it is viewed as a number that is shaped and crystallizes into a more robust form over time. This qualification notwithstanding, there was much skepticism around the veracity of consensus numbers, with many recognizing the shaky foundations upon which they were constructed. As such, consensus can serve as a centrifugal force, something that investment professionals want to distance themselves from, a metric by which self-styled investment elites measure their boldness or distinctiveness vis-à-vis the herds of average investors that are perceived to occupy the majority of space in the investment field.

CONCLUSION

In summary, consensus numbers are a ubiquitous feature of the investment field. Although taken for granted as facts of life, consensus numbers are nonetheless seen for the socially constructed economic phenomenon they are.[18] In this sense, they are not *doxic*, as this would suggest a pre-reflexive attachment. Rather, both buy-side and sell-side actors are well aware that consensus numbers are highly contestable, being the aggregate opinion of sell-side analysts who may or may not update their estimates on a regular basis, who often have to adjust their estimates in order to curry favor with CEOs and CFOs, and who simply may not be that good at financial analysis.

Interestingly, recognition of the noisy, socially constructed nature of consensus numbers does not make them any less powerful in structuring the investment field. Like numbers in other financial arenas, numbers in the investment field have performative effects despite their fabricated[19] or failing[20] character. Both groups identified in this chapter—consensus huggers and alpha seekers—were constantly sense-checking their own estimates and models against consensus numbers. Moreover, those seeking to produce either a more differentiated opinion or a distinct investment thesis relied no less on consensus than did their consensus-hugging counterparts. Both groups were reliant on consensus, albeit in different ways—one centrifugally and the other centripetally.

It is this ubiquitous nature of consensus numbers that makes them an obligatory passage point in the investment field. Whether they are seduced by the illusio of the sell-side analyst as a trusted investment consigliere to asset managers or they are cynically browbeaten into recognizing that sell-side analysis is simply a sweetener to a wider bundle of services offered by investment banks, actors in the investment field cannot avoid consensus numbers even when they try. These numbers provide stability, regularity, and weight to the field, as the metaphor of the anchor (as used by at least one interviewee) connotes. Indeed, although consensus is both centrifugal and centripetal, it is the former that appears to prevail, with social norms and risk aversion dominating the practices of actors; only a minority dare to veer outside of consensus, and even then they limit themselves to predetermined safety zones of 5–10 percent.

Returning to the quote at the beginning of the chapter, if excellence really does imply conformity with the rules of the game, actors in the investment field appear to play the game very well. However, it is crucial to point out that the rules prevailing in the investment field are tacit and operate at odds with the explicit rules of the game. There is a mismatch between the ostensible and the actual roles performed by financial intermediaries. Whereas sell-side analysts self-identify as bloodhounds sniffing out differentiated insights that can move the needle on investment decisions, their institutional reality compromises their ability to do this and instead pushes them to promulgate more anodyne viewpoints and to echo the prepackaged opinions of their peers.

Chapter Five

TECHNOLOGICAL RESISTANCE

IN THIS chapter, we look at the role of technology in the active management space as a way of elucidating the knowledge claims of buy-side and sell-side actors. Technology is important to examine because the rise of passive investing is in many ways a story of leveraging technology at scale in order to make investing accessible to a wider public.[1] Indeed, index investing has been described *as* a new technology per se.[2] Countering the rise of passive investing might therefore require the active community to adopt technology to a greater extent. While technology has had a hugely disruptive impact on financial markets in recent years—particularly in areas such as trade execution, where algorithms and major investments in communications infrastructure have reduced trade latency to microseconds[3]—it seems to have had only a limited impact on the investment process of the active fund community. The ways in which the active fund management community attempts to distinguish winning stocks from losing stocks in its quest for alpha generation have remained stubbornly constant despite the technological maelstrom surrounding it.

In different ways, this also speaks to inertia. Although the focus here is more on highlighting the cognitive structures that persist in the investment field than on the congealed social relations, we recognize that these mutually constitute one another. To that end, a key concept we use in this chapter is *epistemic regime*, which refers to both the knowledge base of a particular group and the way that knowledge is deployed. The concept has been used elsewhere to describe the situated knowledge and strategies of high-frequency traders.[4] We mobilize the concept here in order to frame the beliefs that the active investment community holds about the best way to understand and act on the market. Knowledge is rewarded in professional contexts, and establishing epistemic authority over what constitutes legitimate knowledge in a particular domain is one crucial way in which groups can establish and further cement field position.[5] In this way, groups of actors can establish a symbolic basis for material power.[6]

In this chapter and the next, we zoom out somewhat from the interactions and distinctions previously made between buy-side and sell-side actors, focusing instead on what binds these two subcommunities together. Taken as a whole, both groups are engaged in a joint quest for alpha generation, which is the leitmotif of the active investment community. As tragicomic as this quest might be,[7] it is articulated with great seriousness and no sense of irony by the active investment community. Alpha generation is built upon particular assumptions about how the market works and how investment opportunities may be identified.

We elucidate these assumptions progressively in this chapter via our intellectual probing around the issue of technology, which constitutes an exogenous shock to many fields in society today, from health care to marketing to financial services. Exogenous shocks to fields are boons to researchers because they expose the fundamental structures, both social and cognitive, that hold fields in place. For the purposes of our present enterprise, as the active investment community responds to an increasingly technologically mediated marketplace, its members reveal what they hold dear in terms of their analytical approach. This allows us to identify the key contours of their epistemic regime and assess the extent to which that regime is changing in response to wider changes and challenges in finance and society. Whereas the previous chapters looked at how social structures and social pressures serve as a stabilizing force in the field, in this and subsequent chapters we start to look at how epistemic structures similarly act as a ballast for economic action undertaken by financial intermediaries. Taken together, these perspectives help us build a theory of financial fields that are shaped by both congealed social relations[8] and engrained mental schemata[9]— i.e., by both social and cognitive structures that are far more complicated and more deeply rooted than the individual-level biases to which behavioral finance would limit our attention.[10]

FINANCIAL MARKETS 4.0

Our conversations with respondents vis-à-vis technology ranged from the general to the specific. Initially we asked some very general questions about how technology was impacting the day-to-day activity of the active investment community and how it might do so in the future. This opening gambit elicited a range of responses. For some, technology was seen as something that *complemented* rather than *replaced* human activity. For example, Drew, a sell-side analyst from New York, recognized that technology was having a big impact on financial markets. However, he was clear that human judgment was still ultimately primordial when it came to investment decision-making:

> Whether it's algorithmic trading, whether it's statistically finding anomalies and exploiting them, whether it's the technology to support massive data to discover insights, whether it's the technology for alternative datasets—there is, I think, increasingly this focus on technology to enable the investment process. Which isn't to say that the analysts are becoming less important because to this point there hasn't been something that can fully build itself and then you don't need any human intervention. The analyst is still important, but the technology is becoming increasingly important to sustain that outperformance in a more systematic way instead of just like "Oh, I think this one's going to go up."

The evocation of "outperformance" denotes a focus on alpha generation, which was understood by Drew as fundamentally relying on human analysis and intervention, albeit with technological safeguards built around him. This view implies that human intuition ("Oh, I think this one's going to go up"), although perhaps bolstered by technology, cannot be replaced by it.

This notion that human qualities are inherently superior to machines pervades the active investment community. In some extreme cases, it manifested itself in outright Luddism. For example, there were still many in the investment field who did not embrace technology at all. Melvyn, a buy-side analyst from London, made the following observation:

> But at [this firm], there are still people who just need to print out the research on their table and tell them to read it. They don't know how to use the computer. It's amazing. One of the top fund managers. We need to read from paper. He has a printer and his PA prints things out for him. He still has a paper diary, which is frustrating. Has a little eraser.

While Melvyn spoke with some incredulity about the example, this reflects a broader view that while technological changes are important, it is possible to be a successful analyst or investor in the active space without relying in any major way on technology. This, of course, reflects the nature of our sample of interviewees, who were generally engaged in fundamental analysis and conventional stock picking rather than anything more mathematically complicated, such as statistical arbitrage or quantitative trading. For our interviewees, alpha generation was in many ways an analog enterprise. We now drill down into this further by considering the ways technology does and does not impact what they do.

WHEN TECHNOLOGY *DOESN'T* MATTER: BIG DATA, MACHINE LEARNING, AND ARTIFICIAL INTELLIGENCE

We generated more pointed discussions around technology by asking interviewees how specific innovations related to big data, machine learning, and artificial intelligence—areas that are seemingly reshaping large areas of social and economic life[11]— may be impacting the work of specific buy-side and sell-actors. In both groups, we observed a limited embrace of these phenomena that was coupled with a heavy dose of skepticism vis-à-vis their perceived relevance. We consider the views of both the buy-side and the sell-side in turn.

Buy-Side Views

Big data is commonly understood as high-volume, high-velocity data that require innovative, software-mediated processing.[12] The active investment community understands alternative data as being atypical compared to that used in traditional forms of financial analysis, perhaps because it takes a nonfinancial form (e.g., social network data) or because it looks at financial aspects obliquely (e.g., credit card data).[13] Among our interviewees in the active fund management space, not all embraced big data and alternative datasets with gusto, although they recognized these forms of data as growing phenomena that were displacing traditional forms of research spend. This was explained to us by Alan, an experienced fund manager from Chicago:

I think people are paying for research in different ways. This gets back to third-party stuff. It gets back to paying for the credit card data, and the satellite data, and those sorts of things have replaced the research spend.

Alan's answer comes in the context of paying for research, and the reason given for continued payment is that some sell-side firms use nonfinancial alternative data, data that are outside the traditional domain of knowledge for financial experts. In this case, credit card data offer investment professionals the ability to see trends in spending patterns and identify the resulting impacts on certain industries in coming months. Satellite data might be useful, a number of respondents explained, in observing the activity in shopping mall parking areas or the movement of goods to and from corporate distribution centers. Such observations might bolster the general channel checking that analysts undertake in order to question company earnings projections.

Other buy-side actors were more explicit about the inherent superiority of human judgment and analysis in relation to big data, extolling the virtues of more contextual, subjective judgments. Vaughan (New York) clearly favored the human element:

Yeah, I definitely am on that boat of . . . I think a lot of it's art. And, of course, I had that bias, because I'm a living human being analyst, right. I don't want to be replaced by a machine. But I do think, and I'm proud of this, and I hope this comes across . . . I mean, I've been doing this a while. I really think I know what I'm doing. I just have a large context base that

I mentioned earlier, the foundation of stuff of years of doing it and seeing it—patterns.

Vaughan's quote relates the uniqueness of human judgment to the gradual accumulation of experience that supports the development of a "large context base," the tacit knowledge that many active investors and analysts believe cannot be replaced or duplicated by machines. Vaughan's world of painstakingly put together contextual information supplemented by unique nuggets of insight and interpretation that emerge from his own habitus has formed slowly over time as a result of a constant immersion in the field.

Still others were equally dismissive of recent technological trends in society, recognizing the value of big data in principle but seeing it as the preserve of strictly quantitative funds. For example, Vijay, a buy-side actor in London, in defending traditional fundamental analysis and the raw materials of financial statements upon which this is built,[14] said quite bluntly that big data or AI didn't make sense when you were in charge of only a small portfolio: "It doesn't go with the whole fundamental space. Also, the number of positions, ten to twenty, doesn't really require you to do it."

Quantitative funds might have hundreds or even thousands of positions at any one time, and their investable universe might be the entire market. In that scenario, statistical or machine learning programs that allow analysts to see patterns in stock price movements may be more applicable. Stock pickers such as Vijay, in contrast, were focused on finding anomalies via more intuitive, manual processes in order to differentiate themselves.

Other interviewees explained the irrelevance of alternative data by referencing the strategies and time horizons that fund managers use. For example, Jae, a buy-side analyst from New York, conceded that one could purchase satellite photos of Tesla's parking lot that would probably predict more effectively than he could whether the company was going to meet its production target for the next quarter. However, his fund was less interested in that short-term "quarter-to-quarter" game:

> Our portfolio manager wants us to look at more longer-term types of opportunities where there's something the market's missing that people are not expecting, or the margins are not what people expect, that's going to play out over a two-, three-year time frame.

Jae recognized that machines using big data could find short-term price-sensitive information quite effectively but that ultimately it was the human analyst who could find something "the market's missing" over the longer term. The more subtle subtext here, which again echoes the discourse on the supremacy of human analysis, is that data-heavy strategies are typically short-term and therefore possibly the preserve of hedge funds. All of these examples, many of which we heard in our interviews, noted the relevance of such data to analysis but at the same time highlighted the distance such data collection practices have from the traditional world of active fund management, where data are collected primarily from reports and meetings with management.

Another example of maintaining this distance between the worlds of traditional and alternative data was offered by Crispin, an experienced long-only fund manager in Chicago. While he was aware of big data and alternative data, he found it to be of more relevance to short-term hedge funds:

> I've seen it [alternative data] referenced in some of their [sell-side] pieces. I get calls and emails every week from some type of alternative data vendor. . . . I've looked at it a little bit, and what I've seen, I've come away with is just very short-term-oriented data. Like credit card data, right? . . . Or they'll do website scrapes, scraping data from different websites. Google trend-type data, what people are searching, that type of stuff.

Crispin was clearly aware of data-related changes in the fund management space but didn't feel compelled to alter what he was doing in any meaningful way.

Other buy-side actors regarded alternative data as a potential add-on to their analytical toolbox—but one that was likely to accompany rather than replace existing approaches. This was the response of Steve, a buy-side analyst based in Chicago, when asked if his firm used alternative or big data:

> No, we haven't. We were talking about getting an intern over the summer, and I was like, if I could have somebody that could screen-scrape and stuff like that. Just LinkedIn job postings, things like that, just for little changes.

Screen-scraping LinkedIn job postings from a particular company or industry, like observing shopping malls from satellites, is one way to try to predict activity levels within a particular industry in order to assess likely sales or earnings figures for the next quarter or year. However, our interviewees talked about such alternative data approaches as providing incremental additional insights rather than as offering any game-changing approach to understanding the companies or industries in question.

Some firms on the buy-side have started to work with alternative data, although one interviewee was clear to point out that this stopped short of embracing anything like AI:

> We do stuff like, we track from published databases smart phone sales by country, by model. You know, you can track some of that stuff. You can track Nielsen data for FMCG [fast-moving consumer goods] companies. You can often get reports on sales, for example, online sales versus offline sales, but we haven't entered into the AI era. (Heman, London, buy-side)

Such flirtations with alternative data were seen generally as rather piecemeal and tentative, or "trial and error," or an attempt to "see how it works" (Melvyn, London, buy-side). Again, this gave us the distinct impression technology was something that was happening out there in the ether rather than something that needed to be fully incorporated into investment decision-making in the here and now.

George, a buy-side actor in Chicago, recognized that incorporating new forms of data would involve harnessing more computer science or data science expertise, which was not something that was traditionally part of the active investment habitus:

> We're trying to hire guys that have more . . . that are finance guys that know how to program. Basically, any guy that's my age . . . I'm forty-one . . . any guy who is my age doesn't have that. I think any guy who is twenty-five has a 50–75 percent chance of knowing that. We want to bring in guys who are a little bit better than that. And I think it's just going to change the landscape. Because it's literally a different language that people know. You can aggregate data better. . . . So, if that's true, we need to have people who can come in and aggregate that data.

George highlighted the importance of playing to one's strengths and recognized that traditional fundamental analysis practices were incompatible with big datasets. He also admitted that the different analytical practices were generational and that, as such, it would be very difficult, if not impossible, for traditional active actors to change their practices. To use a social media example, George was from the Facebook generation and would struggle to embrace Instagram or TikTok, and yet he wouldn't completely dismiss the latter two because he recognized that they offered something different that was potentially valuable, although he was in no great rush to invest in their use either.

The belief in the supremacy of human judgment conflicts directly with investment practices that combine statistical reasoning with human stock picking. For example, Swapnesh, a fund manager in London, told us that while he was using more and more technology in his investment process, he held onto the core value of human-centered judgment, unlike more quantitative funds, where he had observed that decisions were driven purely by the numbers:

> My approach is fundamental in the sense that we still go by models that use technology, use statistical tools, but most of the decisions are judgment driven. . . . Just because the model throws up more weight on China or India doesn't mean that you go and invest only in India and China.

Swapnesh did use financial models, as did all of our interviewees, although these were built on Excel rather than anything that required more sophisticated programming like Python.

The challenges that those with traditional active expertise face when technology is introduced are compounded by their firms' organizational structures and conventions. For example, Will was one of the quantitative fund managers that we spoke to in London. He highlighted the challenges of getting senior management to sign off on more advanced technological approaches to analysis—not because the results would not be worthwhile economically but because they didn't understand how these approaches worked. He mentioned that he needed to temper his strategies in order to get their sign-off. For example, he said a business case for investing in technology could not be made by referring to its return potential alone; the process also needed to be intelligible. Because of this, he and his colleagues were precluded from embracing any black box[15] technologies for which they could not establish causal links:

> We have processes that can easily break a hundred gigabyte limits, which is typically what we are allocated in memory. We don't do any black box on it. So typically, no neural nets or deep learning . . . we can't get it past senior management. Because they say that everything we do, they have to understand. And we had one two years ago, which did fantastically well, and I would love to try that, but we can't. And then we did the simplified version of that, which is not a neural net but just a complicated linear regression. And we tried that, and it doesn't make quite as much money on paper as the other one would've made, but at least we understand where the money's coming from.

The strict requirement in Will's firm that management understand the strategy follows directly from the notion of the supremacy of human cognition and intuition over machine power. A purely utilitarian senior manager may have signed off on the neural net version of Will's model because doing so would appear to help generate alpha, but the need to understand what the model was actually doing, which positioned the mechanized model as subservient to the human fund manager, prevented the fund from introducing this technology.

Organizational cultures surrounding active funds were manifested in other ways in relation to technology. Even where interviewees had relevant expertise in computer science or a cognate subject, they didn't fully utilize this knowledge with their funds.

For example, Amal had an MS in computer science from a prestigious university in the United States, which he believes was key to his being hired as a buy-side analyst at a large fund manager in Chicago. However, he noted that in his investment analysis, he used only basic statistical techniques that didn't tap into his deeper knowledge base: "If anything it's basic linear regressions and stuff, nothing like the machine learning etc. If anything, it's just simple correlations and regressions."

Relatedly, some buy-side actors were suspicious of the quality offered by big datasets, which they saw as creating approximations rather than actual, verifiable figures. Jingqi, a buy-side real estate analyst in Chicago, was interested in finding good information on rental income:

> And so a lot of times I find the data is kind of not really a good data, that [it] wastes your time trying to figure out what is going on with the data. I'd rather just go myself to the building and ask what the rent figure is, rather than what alternative data [tell] me. Then I can actually know what is happening.

In addition to such cultural barriers, other constraints on introducing technology were felt acutely in the active community. Karen, a fundamental fund manager in London, was keen to embrace more big data and AI. She was already incorporating some elements of this into her investment process by using predictive modeling and machine learning, but she felt frustrated that her small firm's financial constraints prevented her from doing more in this regard:

KAREN: Yeah, I think big data is something that's going to drive the way forward. As I mentioned earlier on, I said the market structure is changing, and I think in today's world, I think you need a bit of everything. Old-fashioned fundamental analysis is not going to make things work. I think big data is ultimately where I want to see myself, incorporating a larger and larger part in my business.

INTERVIEWER: What's preventing you? Money?

KAREN: Yeah, it's just money, really. We are a very boutique fund. We run a very tight budget unlike the larger platform funds, so I guess, in a way, the fixed cost can be spread over a larger base, whereas we are quite small. We only have six or seven employees, so we're quite small in that sense.

Overall, buy-side actors were rather tentative about technology. They recognized that there were developments out there in big data and AI that might help refine the inputs to their investment process, but they also knew that ultimately the final investment decision would remain with the human investor, who would draw on traditional fundamental forms of analysis rather than programs run by a machine.

Sell-Side Views

As with those on the buy-side, sell-side actors were hesitant about embracing big data and more technologically mediated/ quantitative approaches to investment analysis, although they recognized that a shift was taking place in certain quarters of the investment field. This shift notwithstanding, the sell-side also expressed a worldview that emphasized the irreplaceability of human cognition in the generation of investment knowledge. As Nathan, a sell-side analyst in Chicago, explained:

> I'm focusing more on the unique things that I can do because anybody can go out and buy access to a database. . . . If I can go out and kind of take people to go meet people that they would have, would otherwise never [have] known, or if I can go out and talk to people that they would have no access to, that's a way for me to compete against supercomputers.

Like those we interviewed on the buy-side, Nathan spoke to the unique characteristics of his work and the interpersonal interactions he could facilitate with key actors and decision makers in the field rather than computer-based analyses. This is neither big data nor small data so much as the brokering of in-depth conversations, which he believed would help to provide color or nuance to existing investment theses. Again, we see here how the social and cognitive structures, field and habitus, meet each other in the course of investment knowledge generation.

Even bigger sell-side shops that provided data services on a larger scale than most were only tentatively embracing big data and also expressed the view that machines could only aid the human analyst. This was explained to us by James, who held a senior position in a Chicago subscription-based sell-side firm (i.e., his firm didn't have any ancillary brokerage or investment banking services):

We started as more or less a data company. We've made investments in big data, but in terms of actual predictive analytics with our models, not as much.

Even sell-side firms that effectively see themselves as data companies embrace big data only to agglomerate and collate large volumes of data for their clients, not to use these data with sophisticated analytics tools in order to generate different types of investment insights. While theirs was clearly not an analog process, the absence of predictive analytics was nevertheless indicative of a sell-side shop that had not fully embraced the fourth industrial revolution.

As was the case on the buy-side, there were financial and other constraints on the sell-side's use of big datasets, which Shaun had confronted during his work as a sell-side analyst in New York:

Yeah, the data providers will not sell it to the sell-side (1) because it's extremely costly and (2) if you sell it to a sell-side firm, then it's published to everybody, and you can't sell it to other supply sectors.

Beyond the simple cost-benefit analysis, this quote speaks to the importance of social structures in the investment field. Given that the business model of investment banks is based on publishing research notes for all to see, selling a unique dataset to one sell-side shop may undermine the economic viability of the data vendors. This is not something that a simple price adjustment would fix, somewhat proving the wider sociological point that "it is not prices that determine everything but everything that determines prices."[16]

The role and requisite skills of the sell-side analyst were seen by some as not having changed as a result of technology and increasing volumes of data:

> I think there probably are some "boutiquey" places that would be hiring specific computer people to look at the information flows and how computer program can be set up to kind of exploit that, but that would be a specialist area. As a general sell-side analyst, I think you're still looking for people who would have financial expertise so whether it's accountants or MBAs, I think you still need to understand how accounts and finances and financial modeling works. I don't think that's changed at all. (Ashley, London, sell-side)

Ashley's views in this regard align very closely with the particular types of expertise and knowledge seen as inherent to the active investment community: those sharply focused traditional financial areas rather than computer science or data science. Most of our interviewees saw traditional financial expertise as central to the future success of the active investment community, although it should be recognized that the members of a vocal minority were more fearful for the future of those clinging to this epistemic regime. Indeed, some were quite dismal in their outlook:

> But in general, the market for equity research is collapsing. Buy-side analysts are just a cost center and so many jobs on

both the sell-side and buy-side will be lost to either automation, India, or both. (Christian, London, sell-side)

Christian's views, which raised the dual specters of automation and outsourcing, were not isolated and were echoed on both
the sell-side and the buy-side to some extent. Although not
seen frequently, such views make the widespread attachment to
an epistemic regime that largely eschews technological assis-
tance all the more curious. This is not to say that those in the
active investment community are all Luddites or that they don't
embrace technology at all. Everyone uses email, Bloomberg,
and Excel to significant degrees. However, in their discourses
they position human expertise rather than market devices[17] at
the center of what they do. This proviso notwithstanding, our
interviewees did enthusiastically embrace other forms of technology when doing so was clearly and directly linked to their
compensation, as we now explore.

WHEN TECHNOLOGY *DOES* MATTER:
CLOCKING UP THE BILLABLE HOURS

Customer Relationship Management Systems

While technology, in the form of big data, AI, and machine
learning–driven analysis, was generally seen as largely irrelevant
by our respondents, technology was much more enthusiastically
embraced in some seemingly more obscure or marginal areas of
sell-side analysts' work. For example, one major technology-in-
flected theme that our sell-side respondents brought up was the

introduction of customer relationship management (CRM) systems in recent years. This more proactive approach to technological adoption seems to be driven by new payment methods. The introduction of MiFID II regulation in Europe has had an impact on both European analysts and U.S. analysts who track European companies.[18] Effectively MiFID II has prohibited the bundling of services, requiring the buy-side to pay for research separately rather than paying for it inadvertently through brokerage or other investment banking fees. As we noted in chapter 3, however, we found that this has had a limited impact on resolving conflicts of interest, particularly in the United States. Nonetheless, against this backdrop we find that tracking interactions between the sell-side and the buy-side has become much more pressing as sell-side firms are attempting to move away from treating sell-side research as a free sweetener for a wider bundle of services. This attempt to better track interactions between sell-side analysts and their buy-side clients is evidenced by Nico, a sell-side analyst in New York:

> Normally it's time based, so an analyst will say, "I spent twenty minutes answering three emails from [client X]." I'll look at that, and I'll say, "Okay, well my benchmark is median $1,000 an hour. It took them twenty minutes to do it. I'll make an adjustment: 300 bucks."

This billing process has been facilitated by platforms and CRM systems that track interactions in transparent ways. The evolution in systems was explained to us by Jingqi, a buy-side analyst in New York who had previously worked on the sell-side and so had seen the changes from both angles:

Actually, all the sell-side shops, the big ones, they have their own platform, online platform. It's like a *Wall Street Journal*. You just log into their system, and you can click all the notes they put out, and you can email from within the system . . . to the analysts. Or you can just type out the email and just send [it] to the analysts. So they are all accessible anytime.

This tracking of interactions is facilitated by CRM systems but feeds back directly to the sales team (rather than the research team) at the investment bank in question.[19] As Nathan, a sell-side analyst in Chicago, explained:

It's not coming from me. It's coming from our salespeople like, and this is also . . . one of the other things that's changed. Everything's being recorded now. And this is especially a function of MiFID II. Like I get off the phone with somebody, I'm putting it into our CRM system. Our salespeople get notified right away. Our salespeople pick up the phone, call the trader at the buy-side account, [and] say, "Hey, [analyst A] just spent half an hour talking about x, y, and z. Is there anything else I can help with?" And if they don't eventually start to do business with us, our salespeople, in return, are going to be calling them and saying "Hey, your analysts are using our resources, and they're not paying for it."

Historically it has never really been clear how the sell-side gets paid by the buy-side, something alluded to by Nathan's description. As long as brokerage fees somehow reflected research consumption in the minds of both parties, these relationships would continue with little friction. However, technology-enabled developments around CRM systems, combined with new regulations such as MiFID II, are forcing the buy-side to be much more discerning about those they interact with on the sell-side. This change was described to us by Pierce, a sell-side analyst in Chicago, who had seen the evolution over his approximately twenty-year career:

> I think clients are being much more thoughtful about "Okay, well, internally, they're going to bill me $2,000 for every phone call I have, or every hour-long phone call I have with a sell-side analyst. Or every model I request is going to cost me $50." And I think clients are being more judicious with that. I think they're probably limiting the number of sell-side analysts that they're working with as a result. I think just another side effect is . . . it has been harder to get people on the phone in the last couple of years than it used to be.

At times, working out when a conversation with someone becomes chargeable is rather challenging. Lucia, a sell-side analyst in London, reflects on the point when chatting with a buy-side actor starts to become a "material amount of time" and she needs to start charging for her insights:

> I mean, let me put it like this: if it becomes a material amount of time. So, if you got to use the chat function on Bloomberg, it's usually . . . less than a minute. So you're like, okay, it's

almost too small to bill. It's almost like giving out freebies on a café desk [counter]. But if you walk in and take the entire bowl of freebies, someone is going to need to pay for that.

We were given examples of several scenarios where conversations between the sell-side and the buy-side ended up with the buy-side being charged at some later date. CRM systems are used as a kind of audit trail to justify billing in this regard. They are also used not just by the sell-side but also by the buy-side to track interactions:

> So, we have a CRM, and I think a lot of times we try to match that up with the client's CRM to the extent that they're also tracking it. So if you say, "Hey, I spent six hours on the phone," and they're like "No, we only spent half an hour. What are you talking about?" they'll try to figure that out. (Pierce, Chicago, sell-side)

For what has historically been an extremely murky payment process,[20] technology is facilitating greater transparency and prompting behavioral changes on both the sell-side and the buy-side. This is one example of where technology is being embraced by the active investment community, which is curiously an area that does not fundamentally challenge their epistemic assumptions about alpha generation. The cognitive structures of the active investment community therefore remain robustly unaltered by the exogenous impact of technological change.

Note-Tracking Software

In addition to CRM systems that log meaningful conversations with buy-side clients, a technological innovation that is being embraced by those on the sell-side, in particular, is software that tracks of readership of the research notes they routinely publish. Tracking this readership has become important for billing purposes in the new MiFID II world, and the sell-side now routinely uses sophisticated software packages that help measure readership and consumption of its research notes. Reuben, a buy-side actor in Chicago, explained how this worked, reflecting on his previous employment on the sell-side:

> Yeah. So when I was at [my previous firm], we used Blue-Matrix. BlueMatrix saw when an email was opened. But on your phone, just even if you open the email, that's counting as open. You don't even have to read it. We would also see if . . . we generally put an action statement, maybe a paragraph or two, a couple bullets, then open for the full PDF, the full report. We'd be able to see if someone opened the report. So there's like a front page with a paragraph. But then if you open it . . . so you have sent it to two hundred people, thirty people opened it, fifteen people [opened] the full report. What I've heard about what other sell-side shops have, they'll see how far down you scroll to read a report. We didn't have that capability at [my previous firm]. But that's another interesting level to see how much people are actually consuming.

Reuben's description illustrates how the data gleaned from note-tracking software such as BlueMatrix can be very granular. Such information can be extremely helpful when trying to negotiate payment at the end of a financial period from clients or to push back internally against what might be an unfavorable internal performance review. As Danny, a sell-side analyst in Chicago, explained:

> It helps at the end of the quarter when I get a list saying from this client I didn't get any votes, or sales did not give me any impacts. Some, like Goldman Sachs for instance, they just say, "Here's your total." They don't tell you "This analyst did that, that did that." You just get a number. So, if I look and I don't get allocated anything for my sales, I'm going to go "Here. I published these three things, and these three people each opened every one up, and they opened it up within seven minutes of when I sent the email, so they're reading my research."

Much like academics who become obsessed with their citation scores on Google Scholar or Scopus[21] or social media influencers who to rack up ever greater numbers of followers, equity analysts such as Danny can become quite focused on the extent to which their research is read by different buy-side clients. This is all the more important because their compensation is increasingly directly linked to such information. The capabilities of this note-tracking software, along with the new rules imposed by MiFID II, have made click-throughs—i.e., the number of people who click on an attachment and open the full document—an important performance metric for the sell-side:

> They'll track who's opened an email, [who's looked at] the body text and who's clicked through. To drive revenues you've got to drive click-throughs and you've got to drive client engagement. Whether it's click-throughs, meetings, expert event participation, you know whatever it is. (Albert, London, sell-side)

So click-throughs drive revenues, which, in turn, drive analysts' compensation, making the monetization of research consumption all the more important for the sell-side. When asked to provide numbers on their research consumption, our interviewees offered a wide range of readership stats, from fifteen for one note, which one analyst described as "disappointing," to over one thousand, which that analyst saw as "fantastic." However, Tom, a sell-side analyst in London, pointed out that some banks had not developed their capability in this space as much as others:

> So the bit that we don't have, which a number of other banks do have. . . . This is a system that's supposed to be on its way for at least four or five years now. I suppose they're getting close. The other banks do have versions of it. You can then get very interesting statistics showing how many people not only opened it but how far down the front page they read it, if anybody read as long as page two or page three or page four, what charts they looked at, how long it was open—all this sort of stuff.

In the absence of such granular data, when Tom's firm bills clients for research, it is more an art than a science and is the cause of some of the frustration over the opacity of the sell-side business model that actors in this space experience. Even with such granular data, the bills charged for research consumption are still the outcome of vague, emergent, and negotiated processes. As one interviewee wryly pointed out, nobody really understands the business model of sell-side research, even those working in the space:

> It's the only product that I've ever encountered where you give it to somebody and you hope they pay you for it. That's absolutely what's happening. (Ivan, New York, sell-side, ex-buy-side)

Although tracking research note consumption is increasingly important, there is a value hierarchy that leads sell-side analysts generally to be less interested in whether their notes are read than in whether they are receiving phone calls or emails from clients:

> Honestly when I was at [my previous firm], I paid very little attention to how many people were reading that research. I was only paying attention to inbound calls. When you have a big distribution, big sales force, you tend to get more inbound interest here on a much smaller sales force. That's why there's also parking more focus on our bank making phone calls and following up on emails. (Narendra, New York, sell-side)

This greater emphasis on phone calls or face-to-face interactions has been noted by previous studies[22] and is reflective of the dense social networks in the field that were built on rich narrative exchange and then accreted and congealed. Although at times this in-depth narrative exchange (chapter 3) is compromised by the social nature of evaluation and the pressures to conform to a consensus view (chapter 4), key actors in the field continue to highly prize the former over the latter.

CONCLUSION

In this chapter, we have explored the ways in which the active investment community both resists and embraces technology. Overall, the active investment community is rather ambivalent about greater technological adoption. Ambivalence is, indeed, the key term here, as respondents resisted technology when it appeared to challenge their epistemic regime, as was the case when they discussed big data, alternative data, and AI. In contrast, respondents embraced technology enthusiastically when it afforded opportunities to ensure that compensation was more efficiently allocated, as was the case with CRM systems and note-tracking software.

Our interest in technological innovation has been an indirect way to explore the epistemic structures that underpin practices in the investment management space. Communities tend to reveal what they unconsciously hold dear, or what is doxic, when faced with exogenous shocks to their practices. If doxa is an answer to a question that has not been asked,[23] then the fact that our questions about technology elicited so many responses in defense of existing approaches to doing things suggests to us that doxa was being vocalized. The various responses to the roles that big data and AI might play in their investment process reveal that both the buy-side and the sell-side were wedded to what we characterize here as a hypothesis-driven habitus that privileges small data, unique insights, and interactions with key players in and around specific companies and industries. In the investment field, this approach is referred to as fundamental analysis.[24] The technology of big/alternative data and the machine-learning analytical models that would be required to process such data belongs to a different epistemic regime,[25] so it is viewed with suspicion by fund managers and analysts, who effectively act as "epistemic arbiters"[26] or gatekeepers.

All of this points toward a community that is rather habituated to doing things in a certain way and that is keen to defend the main contours of its epistemic regime. Having now charted these contours and highlighted the importance of the hypothesis-driven habitus, we turn to exploring how this habitus and this regime stand up to more direct challenges to it. In the following chapters, we will probe how the active investment community conceives of and responds to the threats posed by its main rival—the passive investment community. With the rise of passive investing, the legitimacy of the active community's epistemic regime is severely questioned, as is the relevance of the hypothesis-driven habitus. How the active investment community responds to these challenges affords us further insights into the social dynamics of economic fields and, by extension, into how congealed social relations are built upon congealed mental structures.

Chapter Six

THE BIG DOXIC DISTURBANCE

IN CHAPTER 5, we started to see indications that the active investment community was wedded very closely to its existing epistemic regime of small data and bottom-up, fundamental analysis
of stocks. We saw that technology was regarded primarily as
inferior to the human actor and, as such, was positioned as an
aid to rather than a substitute for human decision-making.
Supporting this worldview and indicating that such attitudes
were not reflective of mere Luddism is the fact that actors
embraced technology enthusiastically when it was deployed to
ensure payments for services rendered.

We explore these themes further in this chapter and the next
by showing the discourse that the active investment community produces when faced with the growing threat posed by
passive investing. However, before we delve into the findings
in detail, it is worth taking some time to consider how they
conceive of "the other"[1] that looms large in the minds of active

fund managers and buy-side analysts—the passive investing community. The specter of passive investing haunts the active community in ways that we did not anticipate when embarking on this project. Indeed, in our initial interviews we did not explicitly ask questions about the growth of exchange-traded funds (ETFs) or index funds. These were, however, phenomena that were clearly on the minds of our interviewees, who extemporized freely about the growth of passive investing.

This extemporization reveals something of a *doxic* anxiety. As mentioned earlier, doxa refers to taken-for-granted, unquestioned, pre-reflexive knowledge in the form of particular categories of perception.[2] In chapter 5, we showed that the epistemic regime of the active investment community regards traditional aspects of its work, such as fundamental analysis, small data, and rich interpersonal interactions, as self-evidently and inherently superior to other forms of market analysis, an epistemic position that this community has held for a very long time.[3] As we alluded to in chapter 2, when heterodox discourses emanating from "challenger" groups gain currency in a field,[4] this tends to bring "the dominant agents out of their silence and forces them to produce the defensive discourse of orthodoxy."[5] Moreover, these explanations were proffered in the context of a discussion about passive investing—emerging serendipitously from the respondents rather than the interviewers—which also suggests of some kind of doxic disturbance. Doxa is generally evident when interlocutors can be found "answering 'yes' to a question I have not asked."[6] Therefore, as was the case with our probing of technological adoption in chapter 5, exploring the views of the active investment community vis-à-vis passive investing should reveal the deeper epistemic attachments that the active investment community holds. These attachments form what we have labeled the hypothesis-driven habitus, which, when probed or challenged, comes to the surface, prompting what appears to be a more-or-less anxious attempt to rationalize and explain what normally doesn't need to be explained.

A SHRINKING ECOSYSTEM

When asked a general, open question about what secular, long-term changes were impacting the investment industry, our interviewees opened a veritable can of worms that prompted us to expand our original project—which had been focused more narrowly on the changing interactions between buy-side and sell-side actors—to embrace the broader dynamics that were disrupting active investment. More pertinently the numerous comments about the impact of passive investing on the active investment community opened another window for us into how active investors regarded their epistemic regime when it was threatened by a competing way of knowing and acting on the market.

Data presented in chapter 1 illustrate the extent to which assets under management have flowed out of active investing and into passive investing in recent years. Such trends weigh heavily on the minds of those in the active investing community. In general, respondents on both the buy-side and the sell-side saw a grim future for the active investment community. Numerous interviewees predicted that fees, head counts, and the overall size of the sector would continue to gradually diminish in the foreseeable future. For example, Guido, at a buy-side shop in London, predicted that the active management space, which he recognized had historically had very generous budgets for research, would be able to continue operating only with fewer people, reflecting wider asset outflows (from active and into passive) in the sector:

Active management is becoming harder, so it's an obvious place to cut budgets because the budgets are huge, so either they have to charge less or we use [fewer] people, and I think the way it's going to go is using [fewer] people and having those people that you trust a lot more. So if you assume that outflows are going to continue at sort of 10–15 percent, and that's across the industry, then you probably assume that 10–15 percent year on year is probably going to be knocked off, if not more. Then I think you'll probably find that it will continue cutting away a few of the houses.

According to Guido, a ripple effect of shrinking research budgets would be the closing of asset management firms. Similar views were expressed by Heman, also from the buy-side in London:

Fees are going down, and profitability is going down. Clients are less willing to accept higher fees. The growth of passive has had a big impact.

Heman explained what lay behind shrinking research budgets: lower fees. The lower cost and better performance of passive investing overall have forced those in the active investment community to reduce the fees that they charge their clients in an attempt to prevent more asset outflows.

Sell-side actors had similar anxieties about a shrinking ecosystem. Nathan, a sell-side analyst in Chicago, predicted that the economic squeeze on the buy-side prompted by the growth of passive investing would force some sell-side shops to close:

> I think it is also in large part because of the decline of active management relative to passive management. So there are fewer dollars to go around, and simply being another cog in the wheel, it doesn't get you paid. And so you do have to separate from the pack in order to get those guys who now have a more scarce pool of both attention and commissions and whatever else to speak to you. I think the industry is bifurcating and there are the haves and the have-nots, and the smaller boutique shops, unless they're really good, are just getting demolished. And even at the bigger shops, you have to, you know, you have to really provide something that others aren't.

This quote reflects the perception not only that some sell-side shops would have to close but also that even the better analysts would be forced to work harder in order to capture the attention of an economically diminished buy-side, an insight that is corroborated by emerging research in this space.[7] This has prompted some on the sell-side to start thinking about how they might pivot their services away from the buy-side and toward the companies for which they currently provide research coverage. Indeed, on the basis of the evidence presented in chapter 3, one might argue that the main clients of the sell-side are effectively the companies that they cover.

This dependence on companies rather than the buy-side for income may become stronger as long as active investing keeps losing market share to passive. For example, Alice, a sell-side analyst in London, recognized that fewer dollars would be traveling toward the active investment field in the future due to the growth of passive investing. She explained how she had consequently pivoted her business model away from offering research to fund managers (in the secondary share market) and more toward offering services to companies keen to list on the stock market (the primary share market) for the first time:

> As long as there are companies coming to market, you're good. Of course, that doesn't mean your job is safe forever. Be prepared that you might be left home tomorrow, but I think it's more about IPOs [initial public offerings]. So if there is a primary market, you're fine.

There has always been confusion over whether the sell-side's main clients are actually the buy-side or company management,[8] but the rise of passive investing provided clarity on this issue for Alice, as it pushed her more toward company management.

In addition to widespread concerns about a shrinking economic pool, our interviewees admitted that more and more active funds were losing assets to passive investment because of both fund performance and fee levels. The following comments by Crispin, a buy-side actor in Chicago, were largely representative of this view:

> Active management is losing assets every quarter or every year. . . . So the assets that we've lost over the last five years or so, it had nothing to do with performance. Well, I shouldn't say that. I guess if we were beating the benchmark by 500 basis points [bips] a year or less, five years, there wouldn't be an issue. But we've certainly seen because of fees, they [would] rather pay 20, 30 Bips than 50, 60, 70 Bips to us. We've seen that shift.

The conceptualization implied in this quote, according to which the active and passive investment communities are in direct competition, is a strong driver of the discourse we encountered. Of course, the viewpoint Crispin expressed is corroborated by data on the wider market, which show asset flows have steadily shifted from active fund management to various forms of passive investing in recent years. Although our sampling privileged equity investors and analysts, we also spoke to a limited number of bond fund managers, who told us that fixed-income investors were also being impacted by passive investing, although to a seemingly lesser degree. For example, François, a high-yield-bond fund manager in London, explained that passive investing constituted only around 10 percent of the high-yield market. While he did not see that changing anytime soon, he did concede that there was a lot of fee pressure on his funds because their performance was lagging their relevant indices.

Some studies show that the assets managed by passive fund managers now eclipse those managed by active fund managers.[9] In a recent book analyzing the impact of Jack Bogle—the founder of Vanguard—Eric Balchunas notes that while passive's share of assets under management in the United States was 2 percent in 1993, it was 43 percent in 2020.[10] More recent data from Morningstar show that the market share of equity funds in the United States is now majority passive.[11] In contrast, the rest of the world is lagging in terms of passive but is slowly catching up. Global equity index funds excluding the United States comprise 26 percent of the market according to Morningstar, having climbed steadily from 9 percent in 2008. This trend is likely to continue in the future, although it is interesting how the United States is firmly leading the way.

Estimates of how much of a swing from active to passive has taken place vary, but the general trend is clear to see. Data from the Investment Company Institute show starkly how the growth of passive investing from 2013 onward has come directly at the expense of active investing.[12] Outflows from U.S. active domestic mutual funds were $2.3 trillion from 2013 to 2023, with corresponding asset inflows into U.S. passive domestic mutual funds of $2.5 trillion. It should be borne in mind, however, that overall assets under management in the active space have increased due to growing asset values.[13]

Given these wider trends in the industry, it is therefore perhaps of little surprise that members of the active investment community feel their epistemic regime is being challenged. In fact, the move toward passive investing was seen as logical by many fund managers who conceded that most investors would lose money after active fees were taken into account.

Such concessions, however, were not the product of purely economic reasoning; rather, they were accompanied by numerous comments from our interviewees that were critical of what they saw as a lack of effort on the part of active community members to learn the basics of their purported craft. The following example, which refers to an analyst not knowing that the line-item PP&E stands for Property, Plant & Equipment in company financial statements, was offered by Grant, a buy-side actor in London, to illustrate this sense of frustration:

> There's an analyst who called me from another one of the very big asset aggregators, and we had written a report and that analyst was covering it. And I'm speaking to the person, and the question I get asked is "You are raising a question about PP&E. What is PP&E?" . . . The amount of ignorance on the buy-side is mind blowing, and that's one of the big reasons why I think there is no alpha generation happening, why the industry is moving toward passive. . . . Steve Cohen[14] is right when he says, "The industry has a massive lack of talent." It's just made up of very average people who just don't know what they are doing.

This is a rather stark admission of incompetence in the active investment community, albeit one that does not challenge the epistemic regime of active investing per se so much as it does the competence and quality of many of those who adhere to it. Also of note, underpinning Grant's lament about the reasons for the decline in active investing is the internal distinction that he draws between the untalented and the talented within the community. Grant, who clearly knows what PP&E is, unquestionably places himself in the talented category, much like the distinctions drawn between alpha generators and consensus huggers in chapter 4. Readily drawing distinctions between different groups is a key feature of all fields, financial or otherwise. In the context of finance though, previous qualitative studies of financial intermediaries have noted that it is always "other investors" who are perceived as mediocre and underperforming.[15]

Grant's views were not limited to London or to the mutual fund space within which he worked. A different reason for the shift from active investing to passive, which nevertheless serves the broader narrative about the superiority of human actors, was offered by Murray, a hedge fund manager in Chicago, who had seen a shift in recent years in his space from "20 percent passive to almost 40 percent passive now—especially in trading volume, anyway." At the time of our data collection (primarily in 2019), passive funds were seen as more and more attractive as long as the current bull market lasted. Murray explained to us why this was the case, using the example of a classic hedge-fund strategy of going both long (investing in stocks in the hope they would increase in value) and short (betting against stocks in the hope that they would decrease in value[16]):

> So, if the market is going up 10 percent, let's say you're trying to generate alpha on the longs or the short. You're going to be up 10 percent on your $100 billion long, and you're going to be down 5 percent on your $50 billion short. So you're

going to be up 5 percent. You're always going to underperform the S&P 500. So when the market is up, it's going to outperform you.

Murray's quote is typical of this element of the narrative that implicitly links the continuous bull market with the inability of the active community to show its innate superiority. We will see more explicitly in chapter 7 how those in the active investment community place greater faith in their ability to outperform during bear markets, but for the time being, the key assertion in Murray's example is that the growth in passive funds has been massively facilitated by the current bull market—which was at ten years and counting at the time of our interviews.

Others, such as Christian, a sell-side analyst from New York, saw the challenges faced by both the sell-side and the buy-side as reflective of an irreversible or secular trend, irrespective of whether the bull market turned bearish at some point:[17]

I don't see any reason why this trend toward passive management won't continue even if the market hits the skids, which it eventually will. I still think it's going to take something dramatic for active management to come back. The buy-side continues to shrink, and I think what's left of the sell-side in five years is a much smaller platform, maybe revenues have gotten a little better, and maybe the buy-side just [pays] a little more, at least at the unit level, [than] they do today because there's [fewer] mouths to feed.

Christian described a shrinking ecosystem that produced less bounty to feed the active community. This started with the buy-side actors, who generally fed first, and then impacted the sell-side actors, who were dependent specifically on the active buy-side for food. Our findings, however, indicate that these economic factors are rooted in a more fundamental epistemic regime: namely, the vast majority of the sell-side actors we encountered did not even consider shifting to passive investing strategies—because doing so either would invalidate the relevance of their knowledge or, relatedly, would require them to accept an ethos in which the overarching goal of the practice was to replicate rather than beat the market, to be average rather than exceptional,[18] which would mean there would be no need for differentiated insights from sell-side analysts or for the concierge services they provided.[19]

PASSIVE IS BETTER

Overall, the active investment professionals we spoke to were acutely aware of the threat posed by passive investment vehicles and in many cases saw little that could be done to reverse what they saw as a secular trend. Interestingly, many were so persuaded by the growth of passive investing that they themselves almost sounded like advocates for it. We were surprised to hear a number of actors, on both the sell-side and the buy-side, concede that passive funds were probably the best option for many investors:

I want actives to exist so we have assets, so we have fees, so I have a job. So, I'm biased. Obviously, I think that I have a certain skill level that allows me to beat my benchmark and have pretty decent returns over time and what not. I have to have that view because of the living that I have, but for the average person, and this is now just my personal view, if they just did passives, I'd say, "Go right ahead. I think it's lower fee. Do that." Why should you pay 1 percent, 2 percent, whatever it is for active products? (Vaughan, New York, buy-side)

Vaughan's rather weak defense of active fund management is built entirely upon his own desire to have a job rather than upon its ability to deliver returns for investors or wider arguments about making markets more efficient. His argument alluded to the psychological need for individuals in the active management space to produce rationales that justify their own existence, which we will explore in more detail in chapter 7. This quote is also insightful regarding the active investment community's epistemic regime. Vaughan was quite reflective, to the point of being able to offer an almost perfect example of illusio—a psychological investment or belief in the value of what is pursued in the investment field ("I have to have that view because of the living that I have"). By being able to highlight where and how illusio operates in the field, Vaughan behaved in more reflective and less doxic ways than others and, indeed, must have been experiencing cognitive dissonance as a result. Proclaiming that active funds were necessary while simultaneously conceding that passive funds were better does not sound like a sustainable intellectual position, although we will demonstrate in chapter 7 that the active investment community finds ways to resolve this.

Vaughan's view regarding the greater attractiveness of passive funds was echoed on the other side of the Atlantic by, among others, Charles, a buy-side actor in London:

> You can see the attraction of passive because you're saying "Well, most fund managers don't beat the index, so why am I paying all these high fees when on passive products the fees will be lower?" And in terms of the performance, it is the same or actually slightly superior.

Yet Charles did not have an answer to own question, at least not an answer that justified active investing. Jae, a buy-side actor in New York, said, "For the vast majority of investors, passive is the way to go." He explained that, out of a universe of thousands of active equity funds, there were only five he would consider recommending to his friends. Interestingly none of these five funds were his own.

These reservations about the suitability of active investment, which feature strongly in our findings, are a stark admission of the limitations of active investing's epistemic regime. That is, active investment may be regarded as intellectually superior to replication-based passive investment, but for the needs of most investors, passive would be better. Nevertheless, these reservations are not necessarily admissions of outright defeat. While it is tempting to shout from the rooftops that there are fund managers who would not invest in their own fund or would not recommend their own fund to their friends, this should be tempered somewhat by the barriers preventing ordinary people from investing in many funds:

> By the way, you're not going to get a chance to invest in these funds anyway. . . . There's no way any of us here are investing in them unless you have like $5 million or more to put in. So for the vast majority of people, I think they're better off putting their money in the S&P 500. (Jae, New York, buy-side)

Putting your money in the S&P 500 is shorthand for placing it in an index fund that seeks to track the market, producing beta rather than generating alpha. Index funds generally have very low barriers to entry so retail investors can buy shares in minutes, sometimes investing only pocket change. However, even ignoring barriers to entry for a moment, that Jae would in principle recommend only five funds out of a universe of thousands—not one of which was his own fund—in itself sets off alarm bells about just how much money is being frittered away by active fund managers who have no skin in the game they are playing. No one expressed this more starkly than Ray, whose remarkable views are captured in the following vignette.

VIGNETTE: RAY AND HIS INDEX INVESTMENTS

Arguments extolling the virtues of index funds were made by both U.S. and UK sell-side analysts. In particular, Ray, a sell-side analyst in New York, made this astounding confession during our interview: "All my own money is in index funds."

This was remarkable, given that the ostensible raison d'être of sell-side research is to provide differentiated insights that can feed into the alpha-generating investment decisions of their buy-side clients. Placing all his own money in index funds rather than the active funds that effectively pay for his research demonstrates Ray's profound lack of faith in what he does for a living. We picked up on this in the interview, which is captured in the following exchange:

INTERVIEWER: That's really funny. You are trying to help clients generate alpha, but ultimately you don't believe that it is possible that they can do so. That seems like a massive contradiction to me.

RAY: It is, right? Isn't it interesting? I mean isn't that why Vanguard exists? Like literally, and it is now the largest asset manager in the world by far. And why is all the money moving there and to other index portfolios? I mean, I don't know. I will come across as cynical. It's a good thing it is confidential and off the record. Yeah, how do these active guys make money? They are really bright investors, in general. I think they are really bright, and they are bright in the right way, like check the boxes on schools and tests and things like that. And I think they are very good at convincing other people that they can outperform the market. And so they collect the fees. They erase high-water marks after the downturn, all kinds of things, right.

Ray's disclosure here confirmed many of the criticisms of those in the active fund management industry: they are bright people, they present well to other market players, and they are not completely transparent about whether they beat the market

(*Continued on next page*)

(*Continued from previous page*)

after fees ("erase high-water marks"). However, this still did not explain why he remained motivated to work in a field that, by his own admission, failed to serve society. We therefore probed this further, in what was quite a cheerful exchange:

> INTERVIEWER: But you are part of this process to some extent, in the sense that you are feeding into their process. Do you sort of bounce out of bed in the morning and say, "Hey, I'm going to help these guys fail to generate alpha"?
>
> RAY: No, no, no, I don't. I get out of bed each morning thinking I have an incredibly interesting job because I can learn about China one day and Mexico the next and microfluidics the next day and aircraft engines the next day, and it is a very interesting job. And then debate things with smart people about . . . I almost liken it to being a sports commentator, like we are up in the field commentating on the companies that are battling each other out in the marketplace—on the field and we are commentating on who is going to win and lose by how much.

Much like Vaughan earlier, Ray offered a justification for continuing to work in this space that was very solipsistic: it was an interesting and very stimulating job for him. Additionally, the sports commentator simile was an interesting one, pointing toward someone who enjoys gladiatorial battles but only as a spectator—with all the risks of the battle assumed by others. Also, although he did not say this, we know that he is well compensated, which provides further motivation for him to remain psychologically and emotionally invested in the field.

Ray's confessional is all the more striking because it took place in the belly of the beast, midtown Manhattan, right in the heart of the world's biggest financial center, a center that was built on the triumph of active investment strategies.[20] If capitalism's organic intellectuals[21] lack faith in the principal processes of capital allocation and have to justify their professional activities in terms of their own individual lifestyle benefits rather than their contribution to generating alpha, then this indicates a field that is experiencing not only an exogenous threat in the form of passive investing but also what we refer to here as a doxic disturbance. Such a disturbance occurs when a particular field's dominant epistemic regime, which normally operates under the radar, is thrown into sharp relief by a major threat to those occupying dominant positions in that field. Dominant groups maintain field position by defending orthodoxy,[22] and when such actors cease to defend that orthodoxy, the symbolic basis for material power evaporates,[23] leaving the dominant group vulnerable and susceptible to disadvantageous field repositioning.

A further implication in Ray's vignette is that the responsibility for not generating alpha lay with his buy-side clients in fund management rather than with himself, again proving the point that it is always other investors who are mediocre. This was a view that many on the sell-side expressed in the context of passive investing discussions: they recognized that those in the active investment community mostly underperformed their benchmarks but suggested that this was a burden to be shouldered by the buy-side. The sell-side's job, we were told by numerous sell-side analysts, was to "present ideas and research to help fund managers outperform" (Ashley, London, sell-side). That the buy-side often failed to do so was not something that could be laid at the door of the sell-side. Of course, any impact on the active buy-side would have a concomitant impact on the active sell-side, which was a source of anxiety for the sell-side—but not one that manifested itself in any sense of responsibility. Indeed, taking responsibility for underperformance is not something that the active investment community in general is famous for, which will be the subject of chapter 7.

CONCLUSION

In summary, interviewees confirmed that passive investing was a growing phenomenon in financial markets that was having a real impact on the active investing community in terms of research budgets, staffing, and revenue generation more broadly. Indeed, many interviewees on both the buy-side and the sell-side went so far as to recommend passive investment vehicles instead of their own actively managed funds. Conceptually this demonstrates a recognition that the epistemic regime of the active investment community—which makes certain categorical assumptions about how to interpret and act on the market—is perhaps not as unquestionable as it once was. In other words, our interviewees showed evidence of being doxically disturbed as a result of the exogenous shock that had been caused by the growth of passive investing.

However, despite this doxic disturbance, active fund managers and their advisers still found ways to remain sanguine about the prospects of the active fund management industry. A doxic disturbance might typically lead to a period of questioning and the emergence of a new epistemic regime in the field, along with a new habitus and different rules of the game. However, we have seen no evidence of such adaptation on the part of the active investment community. Ray's and Vaughan's satisfaction with having a job that they found interesting, despite its questionable social utility, is instructive here. In chapter 7, we document and analyze the distinction work that the members of the active investment community have undertaken to help further resolve any cognitive dissonance they may be experiencing as a result of this doxic disturbance.

Chapter Seven

DISTINCTION WORK

IN CHAPTER 6, we highlighted how the specter of passive investing haunts the active investment community, causing what we refer to as a doxic disturbance. This has led many to concede the superiority of passive investing's epistemic regime and to recognize that the passive approach is much more beneficial for your average investor. This must cause cognitive dissonance for those in the active investment community, as they are forced to hold two contradictory views at once.[1] As we show in this chapter, they have resolved this dissonance somewhat by doubling down on their epistemic regime, effectively engaging in a form of epistemic contestation.[2] While they may have conceded that *individual* investors were better served by passive approaches, our respondents argued that the vitality and health of *the market as a whole* required the sell-side to perform fundamental analysis and the buy-side to make active trading decisions. As such, they mounted a spirited defense of active investing. This epistemological chauvinism shows the solidity of the active community's epistemic regime and the extent to which social and mental structures are congealed in the field of investment advice. Once again, inertia is evident in the field. Even when certain ideas and ways of doing things are exposed as ineffectual, the solidity of social and mental structures is such that the field manages to continue pretty much as is.

COMMUNITIES UNDER THREAT

Literature on communities of practice has indicated that when different communities are under threat, they tend to respond in three different ways: first, they reassert a strong identity; second, they disparage those who are threatening them; and, third, they frame certain practices as inaccessible to others, highlighting themselves as the only possible saviors.[3] As we demonstrate here, we find all of these defensive behaviors in the discourse of the active investment community. Given that each of these different forms of defense is effectively drawing discursive distinctions between the active and the passive communities, we refer to them generally as *distinction work.*

In chapter 5, which focused on technology, we touched on the epistemic regime of those operating in the active space and how our respondents remained very attached to this. Theirs is a world of small data, rich interactions between individuals, and microlevel analysis of companies and the key actors that drive value within them. In extolling the virtues of this hypothesis-driven habitus, our respondents effectively were engaging in the first community-level response: reasserting a strong identity. We don't need to revisit those arguments here. Instead, we devote this chapter to listing the various ways in which those in the active community disparage their passive counterparts and frame key practices as inaccessible to passive investment approaches. In terms of disparaging or delegitimizing the passive community, our respondents drew attention to two broad issues: price distortions and the inability of passive approaches to hedge against price falls in a bear market. In terms of framing a practice as inaccessible to the passive community, a number of our respondents drew attention to the area of environmental, social, and governance investing. We discuss each of these in turn. Overall, even though there was widespread recognition among our interviewees that passive investing offered superior investment returns and value for investors (see chapter 6), those same individuals proffered passionate justifications for active investing.

PRICE DISTORTIONS

Beyond the obvious existential threat posed by the growth of passive funds, active managers highlighted day-to-day problems that were caused by what they perceived to be the price distortive effects of index investing. For example, Murray, a hedge fund manager in Chicago, associated passive funds with momentum trading—when price rises beget price rises[4]—which he described as the "bane of his life":

You know the momentum effect? The price momentum in the market is a real thing. Obviously. And I think it gets more prevalent as the years go by, really, with more machines making investment decisions.

What Murray is alluding to here is the way in which algorithms automatically buy stocks. For example, an index fund that tracks the S&P 500 will rebalance periodically in order to ensure that the fund contains a weighted average of all five hundred stocks in the index. If a price increase leads to a concomitant increase in the market capitalization of a stock, that may prompt bots to automatically buy that stock. In turn, more buy orders would lead to yet more (artificial) price increases in the stock, causing the stock price to gain a momentum that is divorced from its underlying fundamentals, such as cash flow, earnings, etc. This causes problems for hedge fund managers such as Murray because stock prices start to move in ways that are harder to predict.

This frustration was echoed by Grant, a hedge fund manager in London, who stated that algorithmically traded stocks caused lots of artificial price inflation, making it hard for him to hold short positions because the price increases would breach his fund's risk tolerance levels:

This stock, for example, for no reason at all suddenly started spiking 5, 10 percent each day for just two weeks. That's it, two weeks, the stock doubled; went from 10 to 20. And then came back promptly within two weeks to 10 back again and then went to 7. So we would have made 30 percent net if we had nothing else wrong. But the point is the way it works is somebody writes a positive note on the stock, one of the robots picks it up, and that picks it up again, so . . . some algorithms, for example the stock has gone up 3 percent in the last three days, buy some more. So it becomes a self-fulfilling prophecy, and that kind of pulls the stock up, up, and up, and at some point, it's like oh, now we have made enough money; turn it down.

Although the passive investing community is the active community's "other," that does not mean that they are separate from one another. Rather, as the philosopher Emmanuel Levinas notes, a subject and their "other" are always mutually constituting one another to some extent.[5] Indeed, Grant's explanation of artificial price inflation demonstrated how the active and passive investment communities interpenetrate one another. Sell-side researchers can write a positive note on a stock, ostensibly for consumption by their active buy-side clients. However, that note will be picked up automatically by a robot, which then creates momentum behind the stock price that is reinforced by swarms of other robots that get swept up in the same direction. Active investors who want to buy the stock are therefore subject to any price rises that have been prompted by this process. This is not to say that equity researchers necessarily run behind passive funds in terms of their recommendations and advice;[6] rather, the two exist in a dialectical, mutually constitutive relationship.

Price distortions were perceived to cause problems not just for the buy-side but for the sell-side too, as analysts may struggle to offer plausible reasons for price spikes or drops to their fund manager clients. As Drew, a sell-side analyst in New York, explained:

> Algorithmic and fast money is another huge topic because it's changing the dynamics of the stocks that we cover . . . it's creating these more drastic changes in stock prices. . . . If a client calls, they're like "Why is this stock down 10 percent?" They miss margins or something, modestly, and it's like "Ah, I don't know." Or maybe it's like the algorithms or whatever; it's a very common thing.

Drew's explanation alluded to the relatively opaque nature of how algorithms work, with the sell-side struggling to see what lay behind drastic changes in stock prices. Back on the buy-side, Felix (London) argued that the momentum created by exchange-traded funds (ETFs) and algorithmically oriented funds meant that everyone ended up chasing the same opportunities, making it harder to outperform:

> So, what I see is that everybody's following the same, everybody's chasing the same stocks, everybody's chasing the same investment ideas and not only this year, the year before, and the year before. So maybe the whole economic and financial environment is prompting active investors to follow the same idea, and there is little outperformance.

In this respect, Felix effectively blamed passive investing approaches for the active community's failure to generate alpha.

This blame game has become a common trope within the active investment community.[7] Indeed, blaming passive investing for active's woes was a recurring theme from our buy-side respondents. For example, Steve (Chicago) noted that passive investing's impact on price distortion was so significant that his fund had decided to avoid investing in stocks that were targeted by robot ETFs because it was, in his view, impossible to make sense of the price changes that these EFT trades cause:

> It's basically just from the informational perspective and understanding risks, versus we wouldn't invest in something that is tied to a robot ETF, even though they don't have any robotics, so that it might move wonky, different than what you would expect.

Steve went on to explain that while robot ETFs caused short-term price distortions and it was hard for active funds to make sense of these, "over time, it all corrects"—evincing an underlying belief in efficient markets. This is a view clearly shared by many others in the active investment community, as the following quote from Jaymal, an equity analyst in London, illustrates:

> The sense I get is that increasingly there's more volatility on the day of results and a beat or miss that would have historically been a 2 or 3 percent share price move appears now to be more like a 5 percent share price move. My suspicion is that that reflects the relative liquidity in these things versus active and versus passive. And obviously passive holdings

of these companies increase the proportion of the free float that's out there.

Although passive funds tend to trade less than active funds, Jaymal nevertheless indicated that passive investing increased the free float (the proportion of shares that are publicly tradeable), which, in his view, increased the scope for price distortions.

PRICE DISCOVERY

Many of our respondents lamented the price distortions that they perceived as being caused by index funds and castigated the passive community for this. However, some respondents saw the distortive effects of passive funds as potential sources of value for the active community and for society more broadly. For example, Louis, a buy-side actor in Chicago, explained the importance of identifying firms that were about to be picked up by ETFs: "When you've got a company that is looking to, that is on the cusp of entering an index, you gotta pay attention to that." Once a firm enters an index, the interest in it increases significantly because of the demand created for its stock by ETFs and index funds. Active managers can also take advantage of the price surges that tend to follow inclusion in an index, as Harold, a buy-side actor in London, described:

Actually, the growth of passive represents perhaps an opportunity for us, which I hadn't really appreciated before. We've actually been more interested, at the moment, in the strategies and the inefficiencies that would come out of that.

Harold was expressing a canonical viewpoint in financial markets: namely, that inefficiencies create opportunities for price discovery. *Price discovery* denotes the establishment of the proper price or intrinsic value of a particular stock, which is presumed to emerge in the market when buyers and sellers engage in multiple transactions until consensus is reached on price. Key to this process, the theory goes, is having active players in markets. The more active players there are, the more effective price discovery is presumed to be.[8] This process of price discovery, insofar as it happens, is beneficial for those engaged in it, as they can go long or short on mispriced securities. The process of price discovery is also presented by economic theorists as beneficial for the market and society as a whole, as it increases efficiency and ensures the fair allocation of resources. Such viewpoints were reflected by our interviewees, as illustrated in this vignette of Geoff and his drug research.

VIGNETTE: GEOFF'S DRUG RESEARCH

The notion that price distortions create opportunities for savvy active players speaks to a price discovery function that the active community perceives itself as performing for the market more broadly. For example, Geoff, a sell-side analyst in London, illustrated at length the ways in which a diligent analyst such as himself could, through in-depth, patient research, identify inflection points in stocks that a passive investment vehicle would never be able to pick up. The example he gave us was of a company running a trial for a gene therapy that aimed to slow down degenerative blindness. Given the complexity of his example, we include it here at length:

> France is already allowing patients to use it [the gene therapy] on an emergency basis. And it's in registration in Europe so the European regulator's looking at it, and they're running a trial in the U.S., and that trial is due to report out in the next three months. Now we think that trial will fail because the gene therapy, when it's put into one eye, they don't inject into the other eye and that's your placebo eye. But what we think is happening is the gene therapy is transmitting to the other eye—to the placebo eye. So we don't think they're going to see a difference with [the] placebo. So we think the study in the U.S. will fail, although the treatment's good. So the European regulators looked at it and said, "Hang on. These patients, they're not becoming blind as quickly. We're not really sure why. But with your drug, they're not becoming as blind as quickly." And, unfortunately, the element of the trial design is flawed. So what we expect to do is announce that the drug's failed in this U.S. study, stock to come up, and then that becomes a great opportunity to take advantage of European sales and then the FDA and the U.S. regulators are gonna have to turn around at some point and say, "We've got to work out how we get this, how we deal with this issue of transmission because patients are going blind for no reason." So, you know, the

(Continued on next page)

(Continued from previous page)

> client's asking us "What's gonna happen to the stock?"
> You know, I'm pretty sure this is a good drug. I've spoken
> to a lot of patients that have benefited from it. . . . No
> electronic trader could pick that kind of analysis up. You
> just have to work your way through it.
>
> Geoff's example highlighted the perceived importance of
> undertaking proprietary research in order to determine the like-
> lihood of a particular stock taking off or not. Passive and even
> active quantitative strategies, which he pointed out in a catch-
> all reference to an "electronic trader," cannot incorporate this
> sort of background channel checking because—at least in the
> case of passive strategies—they simply jump into a stock once
> it has already surged enough to get into the index. As a result,
> Geoff saw the active investment community as both being able
> to benefit from such strategies and serving a wider price discov-
> ery function for the rest of the market.

Geoff drew attention to the way in which sell-side analysts
are essential in providing price corrections.[9] Other equity analysts, such as Phillip (London), expressed similar views:

And I think that we can do a lot on the sell side, particularly at times when price formation is inefficient or in doubt.
And whether that's an IPO [initial public offering] situation,
whether that is heightened uncertainty about the future cash
flows in a stock . . . then we can really add value because of
those events. You know, if you've got a strong thesis about

why a stock should be priced a certain way, and it turns out to be valid, that can add very clear value that passive isn't going to compete with.

Phillip talked specifically about being able to do something he believed passive could not do that could provide direct value for clients. In the preceding vignette, Geoff also talked about providing direct value for clients, although he also alluded to the wider service that sell-side analysts perform for the market and for society more generally. Other sell-side analysts went further with this societal benefit argument. For example, Ashley (London) saw sell-side analysts as a public good, comparing himself and his sell-side colleagues to streetlights:

> I think that a lot of the role of a sell-side analyst is almost like a public good. There is obviously the specific kind of functions you perform that can be priced and quantified and charged for. But you are kind of, who's paying for streetlights? You need them, but if they're all switched off, you suddenly find a lot more cost and accidents, and I think there's an element to the sell-side role that is very much part of that public-sector, public good–type function.

The "cost and accidents" metaphor denotes the price distortions that are caused by investment strategies that automatically buy assets without doing any due diligence via fundamental analysis. Extending this argument further, Ashley argued that the analysts' "streetlight" function was even more valuable in an ETF-driven market than it had been previously:

From a market efficiency and a kind of analysis point of view, there's a more momentum-driven market. As an analyst, you're looking for individual stock ideas and more kind of attuned to active fund management. So how does that play out? In theory, it should mean that we're even more valued because we can spot those opportunities and see what's happening on individual stock levels, whereas if you put money into an ETF, if a stock's gone up 2 percent, you're going to see that ETF go up, more money flows into it, and maybe the valuations start to become even more inefficient.

In this respect, Ashley saw himself and other sell-side analysts like him as essential to the efficient functioning of the market, as he justified his role in abstract, disinterested, and societal terms. Buy-side actors also made arguments in terms of the active community's role in price discovery, although they tended to be less disinterested and noble. Instead, they had a narrower and more opportunistic frame of "What can passive do for me?"—as indicated by Grant, a buy-side actor in London:

> But then there is also the argument that at some point, if everyone goes passive, who's doing price discovery? And does it then actually swing back and become easier for active managers? Now, I've seen no evidence that that's true, but I understand the idea that if the world goes passive, you want to be the one active manager out there because there's suddenly going to be opportunities for you.

In contrast to Ashley's seemingly selfless presentation of sell-side analysts as a public good, Grant's discourse took on a dog-eat-dog tenor, highlighting the opportunities that existed for active fund managers in a passive world full of mispriced stocks. In both cases though, the role of the active community in price discovery was clearly spelled out and presented as a strong justification for the active community's continued relevance.

In sum, despite the growth of passive investing and the overall case against active investment strategies, these specific examples of price inefficiencies being uncovered by active researchers were cited as evidence of the continued relevance of the active investment field. The passive investment field was presented not only as unable to perform price discovery but also as actually the cause of many price distortions in the first place. In some instances, passive investing was blamed for being one of the main reasons that the active community failed to generate alpha.

JUST WAIT AND SEE WHAT
THE BEAR MARKET BRINGS!

A further form of distinction work was undertaken by our respondents when they discussed wider market conditions. As explained earlier in the chapter by Murray. a buy-side actor in Chicago, bull markets created conditions in which it was difficult to beat passive funds, particularly for hedge funds, which, by definition, are always simultaneously going both short and long. The corollary of this *cri de coeur* is that bear markets, which are commonly characterized by a prolonged drop in stock prices, offer more propitious circumstances for alpha generation.

Specifically, the passive community was seen as being able to operate only in certain market conditions and thereby as being of limited utility. Indeed, speaking in spring 2019, Mahesh, a buy-side actor in Chicago, explained that he was looking forward to the next economic downturn because passive funds would have no strategy to hedge their way out of it. Indeed, he welcomed the growth of passive funds, as this presented asset managers like him with "more lambs to the slaughter." In less biblical language, Jae, a buy-side actor in New York, similarly welcomed the growth of passive funds because these, in his view, led to less value being "priced in." This was an extension of the price discovery argument discussed earlier. Effectively Jae's argument was that bear markets contained even more mispriced securities than bull markets did, meaning that there would be opportunities for savvy active investors like himself. In turn, he saw this as an opportunity for the alpha generators to reestablish themselves in the investment field:

> I don't know what the tipping point is. People are saying that as more flows into passive, the hope is that we can eventually go back to an era. . . . It may not be what it was twenty years ago, maybe like ten years ago. We can go back to an era where it would be a lot more easy to make money. Less people playing, and the return, the alpha, could be bigger in the space.

Jae yearned for how things used to be, echoing wider views that there might be too much passive money in markets already,[10] although the asset flows toward passive investing[11] imply that this is not a majority view. This wider debate notwithstanding, other buy-side actors, such as Melvyn in London, expressed hope that active funds would be proven more valuable when a bear market came around:

> And I'm not quite sure just personally whether momentum and [inaudible] trading will work in the downturn because we had an upturn and it's all about chasing the up cycle. But whether the old rhythm will figure out when things start collapsing, liquidity will dry up, the machine cannot predict how fast. There is no price for certain things and what they would do. So I don't know whether in a bear market that [passive] would be as popular as now.

The distinction drawn here by Melvin and others between bull and bear markets serves to position the passive community as helpful for investors in the former but not the latter. Sell-side analysts who also clung to this notion included Geoff, a sell-side analyst in London who was interviewed in the summer of 2021, about fifteen months into the Covid-19 pandemic:

> Um, well, the problem is we're still in a bull market in my mind, right? When I talked about going into a bear market, I'm thinking about maybe a three- to five-year bear market, and you would only see that maybe twelve to eighteen months in, we're nowhere near—in terms of the timescale of Covid, the stock market has already gone past Covid. So it's written it off. And actually, if anything, people are now even

more obsessed with the stock market. You probably see more and more money going into passive right now. So, you know, you will need to test that thesis when we've really got into a bear market.

Geoff is evincing strong defensiveness around active funds here, arguing that, in his view the market turbulence had not yet gone on for long enough for passive funds to start declining.

Albert, another sell-side analyst in London who was interviewed around the same time as Geoff, had a slightly different view: he saw the then current climate as an ideal opportunity for the active investment community to test its mettle against passive strategies:

> And I think it'll be very interesting if we're going through a period now that—who knows quite how long it'll last—but it does clearly offer the buy-side much in the way of alpha generation opportunities. I think the argument that might have been valid twelve to twenty-four months ago—that it's very hard to generate alpha against passives—is just not, you know, as clearly the case right now.

Geoff and Albert disagreed over whether or not they were currently in a bear market and, by extension, whether the active community was in the best position to prove its worth. These differences notwithstanding, evidence of how the active fund community performed during Covid-19—and particularly in 2022, when most stock markets lost value—suggests that a majority of active fund managers still underperformed their benchmarks[12] and the flows from active to passive increased during that time.[13] Indeed, comparing the last three periods when the U.S. stock market experienced major impacts (2008, 2018, and 2020), Eric Balchunas presents data that show the same trends of chronic underperformance by active managers and of investors fleeing the active space.[14] His explanation for the latter is threefold: (1) older investors abandon active management in downturns because they are close to retirement and don't want to risk losing any gains accumulated, (2) a bear market frees those who have invested in active funds to use losses to offset any capital gains they have realized, and (3) there is always a baseline of outflows going from high-cost (active) to low-cost (passive) funds that is immune to market conditions.

Despite such evidence, active field actors label passive investment strategies as risky when prices are generally in decline: passive field actors have no ability to predict when this might happen or to hedge against such eventualities because they are generally "long-only" in orientation.

ONLY ACTIVE CAN DO ETHICAL INVESTING

A further form of distinction work, which was seen more among financial actors in Britain than in the United States, related to the respective abilities of active and passive investing to incorporate meaningful environmental, social, and governance (ESG) factors into investment strategies.[15] Although becoming more and more commonplace in the UK and Europe, ESG is seen by many in the United States as an unwelcome constraint on return maximization or even a breach of fiduciary duty except in certain circumstances.[16] Indeed, this has become a political issue, with President Joe Biden using his presidential veto to reject a measure passed by Congress that would have overturned a U.S. Labor Department rule making it easier for fund managers to consider ESG criteria in their investment processes.[17]

Whether ESG is desirable or not is clearly a politically charged issue, and we are certainly not presenting it here as a self-evidently desirable course of action to take. Indeed, detractors of what was once called corporate social responsibility but what now goes by ESG (old wine, new bottles?) suggest it is an ideologically mischievous movement that might actually move society further away from a solution to the ecological crisis and growing social inequality.[18] Indeed, Bloomberg concedes that ESG scoring metrics "don't measure a company's impact on the Earth and society" but rather "gauge the opposite: the potential impact of the world on the company and its shareholders."[19] That is, ESG is not intended to help protect the environment from companies but rather to help protect companies from the environment.[20] Therefore, as an aside we would caution against an enthusiastic embrace of ESG as any kind of solution to social and environmental ills, as such corporate-led movements might well constitute a step in the wrong direction.[21]

Irrespective of the merits or ideological obfuscations of ESG, it is of interest to us here because it was framed as a practice area that was inaccessible to the passive community. Thus, it constitutes another form of defensive distinction work consistent with a community that is feeling threatened. As indicated by Gustav, a buy-side actor in London, one of the key phenomena driving the growth of the assets under management (AUM) by his fund—which he admitted was underperforming relative to benchmarks—was his firm's willingness to deal with ESG issues:

> When we started about two years ago, we were kind of asked for ESG for the first time. At the time, however, it was just a small proportion of investors that wanted ESG. Nowadays, most people actually want it. And the main reason why we have been able to grow our assets was because of ESG. It wasn't because of the systematic return prediction or alpha process; it was because of ESG.

Gustav described himself a "systematic" investor, following quantitative approaches to identify key factors in alpha generation.[22] Although he had narrowly failed to beat his benchmarks in recent years, this didn't prevent him from growing AUM because of his firm's incorporation of ESG into its portfolio selection. His views on ESG as an opportunity for the active community were echoed by those using a more fundamentalist approach. For example, Angus, another buy-side actor in London, described how ESG and engagement (engaging corporate boards through mechanisms such as voting at annual general meetings and proposing shareholder resolutions) were his fund's "secret sauce":

> Yeah, I think ESG and engagement are fundamental to what makes us a good active manager. And actually, I would go as far as to say that engagement is our secret sauce. . . . And I would, arguably, I would say that is the edge. And it's the one

thing that cannot be commoditized by the passives and can't be modeled.

As head of investment, Angus effectively oversaw a group of fund managers in his firm. He went on to explain the various ways in which engagement worked for them:

> It's about going and talking to the C-Suite, it's about talking to the board, about setting objectives and having stepping stones, measurable stepping stones, to get to those objectives. We'll only ever have two or three things that we're talking to a company about. There might be one sort of overall, I call it a guardrail activity, which might be around governance. So, it might be board composition or exec pay . . . we vote against their executive pay, even if that's not the issue. The issue is you're emitting too much carbon, but you won't take us seriously and you won't listen to us; then we're going to vote against your executive pay.

The detailed explanation around engagement here is designed to hammer home the point that passive investment vehicles, even if incorporating some ESG screening criteria, are not designed to undertake this form of corporate cajoling. We were told that if investors wanted to be ethical, they would have to enlist the help of the active community. Other fund managers expressed similar views:

> People talk about decarbonizing their portfolio and the need to address climate change, either to help solve climate

change or to take advantage of it; it isn't easy to get to a truly passive solution. (Grant, London, buy-side)

However, the notion that active fund management had an advantage over passive investment vehicles in the ESG space was keenly contested by Raymond, an independent pension trustee adviser in London:

> I find that incredibly rich of the active fund industry, which [has] largely for decades cared nothing about stewardship, that, all of a sudden, you know, now we know about climate change. And, you know, they're under this massive existential threat from passive. They're saying "Oh. You've got to be an active investor to ensure that companies are being held to account on issues like the environment and society and so on."

Beyond pointing out what he saw as the hypocrisy of the active investment community on this issue, Raymond argued that passive investing might actually offer a better means by which to influence corporate behavior:

> If you're an active manager and you don't like what the board is doing, you can just throw the toys out—take the toys away if you like. But if you're a passive manager [and] your mandate requires you to carry on investing in those funds, you have no choice but to carry on engaging.

The implication here is that an obvious solution for active funds is to "take the toys away" (divest), but passive funds, which are tied into certain companies due to index tracking principles, might have longer-term mandates and potentially more influence over corporate boards. Similar views have been expressed by key thinkers in the passive investing space who point to the extensive engagement undertaken by large passive investors such as Blackrock and Vanguard.[23] Such criticisms notwithstanding, ESG appears to have emerged as a key justification for the continued allocation of capital to the active fund management industry, at least according to the active investment community itself.

CONCLUSION

In this chapter, we have outlined the different discursive strategies that the active community articulates in order to defend itself against the big doxic disturbance posed by the seismic growth of passive investing. Consistent with how communities often react when they are under threat,[24] we have observed active investors doubling down and reasserting their identity, disparaging passive investors, and framing certain practices such as ESG as inaccessible to passive investors. Each of these forms of distinction work is contestable: for example, many passive firms have large ESG engagement teams, and there is bountiful evidence suggesting that active strategies fare even worse in bear than in bull markets.[25] Indeed, it is interesting to note that our interviewees did not try to defend their position in terms of performance, which is the most important measure in the market. The key conceptual insight here is that there appears to be little in the way of adjustment to the habitus of active community members despite the seismic growth of index investing in recent years. In this respect, arguments that effectively amount to "let's keep on keeping on" are indicative of a community that has hunkered down and is refusing to adapt to an external world that is being reshaped along different epistemic parameters.[26]

Research has shown that the passive community is very active in ensuring that its investors behave passively, discouraging them from tinkering with portfolios and ensuring that they remain on the efficient frontier of modern portfolio theory.[27] In contrast, we have shown here how the active community is rather passive about its own decline relative to index investing, falling back on the well-established dispositions and practices of its actors—in effect, fighting this threat with more of the same. The threat of passive therefore does not create a doxic disturbance that is as big as it might be—it's more of a tremor than an earthquake. Alternatively, if the growth of passive investing *is* more seismic in its scope, which the data seem to suggest it is, then those in the active community have effectively sheltered themselves behind some very well-constructed epistemic ramparts that are capable of intellectually withstanding whatever is thrown at them. This doesn't mean that they will survive into the future though—merely that their self-belief and self-regard are very strong. In this respect, in addition to the social inertia we documented earlier in the book, we suggest that the active investment community exhibits strong indications of *epistemic inertia*—the continued attachment to an existing epistemic regime in the face of changing field conditions.[28]

In the conclusion, we will discuss the main findings of the book and reflect on how social inertia and epistemic inertia are interrelated and how congealed social relations and ossified mental structures feed on one another and manage to persist in economic domains that pride themselves on innovation, disruption, and fresh thinking. This will lead us to develop a theory of inertia in financial markets that is actively and robustly cultivated: purposeful inertia. The word *purposeful* here denotes two things: membership in the active fund management community, which is driven by an ostensible (although seemingly impossible) purpose to generate alpha, and the amount of effort that goes into defending the existing social relations and epistemic regime that support the active community's still advantageous field position.

CONCLUSION

PURPOSEFUL INERTIA IN FINANCIAL MARKETS

WE CONCLUDE this book by drawing together and synthesizing the insights from the previous chapters, returning also to the themes identified in the introduction and chapter 2. Broadly speaking, the insights gleaned from the previous chapters go some way toward establishing a more solid conceptual basis for what David Hirshleifer would call social finance,[1] which goes beyond both mainstream finance theory's penchant for economic frames and behavioral finance's marginally more expansive approach to understanding economic action.[2] Essentially the foregoing chapters demonstrate the importance of understanding the work of financial intermediaries from a broader social perspective, drawing on sociological theory and paying empirical attention to the social dynamics, cultural templates, and epistemologies that guide economic action.

Chapters 3 and 4 show the importance of social inertia to the functioning of financial markets, whereas chapters 5, 6, and 7 demonstrate the persistence of an epistemic inertia that characterizes the active fund management community in the face of a seemingly existential threat. These two concepts are interrelated. For example, the epistemic regime of active fund management is long-standing and institutionally embedded. In a theoretically efficient market, this regime would have been swept away and replaced by ideas that encourage better resource allocation. That these ideas and those who embody them have managed to retain such prominent, well-remunerated positions in financial markets is indicative of the extent to which social relations are congealed in economic fields.[3] Indeed, while it is tempting to view the continued rise of index investing as a sign that the market is slowly awakening to better ideas, it is equally plausible to suggest that active fund management—which continues to grow in terms of absolute assets under management globally, even if it is losing market share—remains remarkably successful in carving out a role for itself and convincing investors to place their faith in it. Overall, this leads to a view of financial markets as characterized by inertial tendencies, with social and epistemic dynamics reinforcing one another in dialectical fashion.[4]

PURPOSEFUL INERTIA

The inertia we observed, whether social or epistemic, is not the product of an attritional battle between opposing groups vying for epistemic authority, as previous research on financial regulation has shown.[5] The active and passive communities are locked in a head-to-head battle to be sure, but this does not prevent market share from moving in favor of one community or another, much the way regulatory initiatives often fail due to a lack of resolution between competing parties. Nor is this inertia mere laziness or lethargy on the part of financial intermediaries, whom we observe working long hours and producing both spirited discourses about their own job roles and keen observations on the dynamics of the field around them. The actors we encountered did not do what they did because of the dull compulsion of economic relations.[6] Rather, they were seemingly very enthusiastic about what they did and motivated to continue doing it, thereby seeking ways to counter the growing threat of passive investing strategies. The inertia we observed is therefore not so much a passive response to an existential threat as a standard response by a group of actors who extoll the virtues of orthodox discourse in an attempt to maintain field position.[7] In this respect, inertia—being the continued attachment to a certain epistemic regime that is itself embedded in long-standing, sticky social relationships—is purposefully and dynamically reproduced.

Path dependency, habit, and routine clearly also explain congealed social and cognitive structures in the investment field, but actors were reflective about these, brought them to the surface during our conversations, and found ways to explain why certain relationships remained sticky or why ossified ideas were still pursued. In this respect, the investment field is no different from other economic fields, where certain cultural norms[8] and forms of social capital[9] act simultaneously as important drivers of stability and as barriers to change and innovation. For example, the existing forms of homophily in the field surely make it more difficult for field-wide demographic change, such as, for example, gender diversification, to occur.

It would seem that some of the key relationships between the actors that structure the investment field, which in some respects appear to have outlived their useful economic lives, cannot be disrupted. We offer some summary reflections here as to why this is the case. First, disrupting existing relationships would lead to internal friction within firms, as when a junior analyst undermines their superiors, so a decision is made not to rock the boat or push for change. Second, even when sell-side analysts are lambasted for offering little or no value in terms of research insights, they are kept on a buy-side roster because their brokerage colleagues are helpful or because the buy-side is concerned about missing out on future equity placements brokered by the sell-side firms for which these analysts work. Third, there is basic human empathy, which discourages buy-side actors from cutting people loose when they like and have long-standing relationships with them. These various reasons were all proffered by buy-side respondents and are suggestive of a level of reflection and consciousness around the sticky nature of social relationships in the field. As such, the social inertia that we observed is not merely the nonagentic outcome of habit, routine, and path dependency, even if these factors are also present; it is also the product of purposeful social action. Indeed, on the basis of the evidence presented in this book, we argue that habits and routines are often purposefully enacted in ways that create future path dependencies in the field.

The purposeful nature of inertia is as true for epistemic inertia as it is for social inertia. Attachment to the "defensive discourse of orthodoxy"[10] is to be expected from an incumbent group that is trying to maintain field position.[11] When faced with the heterodox epistemic regime associated with their challenger, passive investing, our respondents expressed real ambivalence, conceding the value of this but hunkering down while making a case for the continued relevance of their own epistemic regime and its attendant features of fundamental analysis, small data, and the rich narrative exchange that emanates from interpersonal encounters. This ambivalence, while indicative of a certain cognitive dissonance on one level, is also indicative of a community that is aware of and reflective about the potential shortcomings of its own epistemic regime. That its members then go on to defend what might be characterized as ossified ideas is nonetheless a purposeful act and all the more contentious for being so. There is an epistemic struggle going on between orthodoxy (the active epistemic regime) and heterodoxy (the passive epistemic regime), the stakes of which are high in terms of field position in the investment space, along with the concomitant symbolic and material rewards that go with this. In other words, our respondents are proselytizers of orthodox discourse, which is again a purposeful act.

This is not to say that the promulgation of that discourse is a purely cynical or instrumental choice. The very nature of orthodoxy presupposes some sort of tacit acceptance of or deep-rooted attachment to that discourse, something that is prereflexive.[12] As such, the active community's defense of its epistemic regime does have something of a taken-for-granted aspect to it, in which that regime is presented as a self-evidently desirable way of doing things. Otherwise, these respondents would not be able to resolve the cognitive dissonance that they may be experiencing as a result of the growing number of assets under management held by the passive community. On this psychological dynamic, Max Weber's rumination on elites is quite instructive:

> When a man who is happy compares his position with that of one who is unhappy, he is not content with the fact of his happiness, but desires something more, namely the right to this happiness, the consciousness that he has earned his good fortune, in contrast to the unfortunate One who must equally have earned his misfortune. Our everyday experience proves that there exists just such a need for psychic comfort about the legitimacy or deservedness of one's happiness, whether this involves political success, superior economic status, bodily health, success in the game of love, or anything else.[13]

This is helpful in explaining why actors such as Vaughan and Ray (chapter 6) could remain so buoyant about working in the active investment space even while advocating index funds. That is, those occupying the command posts of the economy,[14] which asset managers effectively do in what has been dubbed "asset manager capitalism,"[15] have a psychological need not only to occupy a dominant field position but also to feel good and righteous about it, resolving any cognitive dissonance they may be experiencing as a result of the rise of passive investing.

This goes some way toward explaining the mental gymnastics that active field members undertake when justifying their own field position.

Overall, the seemingly contradictory mental position that respondents take vis-à-vis the rise of passive investing and the frustration that they express with existing social relations in the field are resolved or assuaged by a combination of strategic calculation, perceived necessity, social pressure, blind adherence to routine, and psychic comfort. Inertia is therefore comprised of myriad dynamics, both conscious and unconscious.

RETHINKING FINANCIAL MARKETS

In addition to this new notion of purposeful inertia, we see a key contribution of this book as a new conceptualization of financial markets and the financial intermediaries that populate them. We have drawn on various concepts in the course of the book, including field, habitus, and doxa from Pierre Bourdieu; congealed social relations and strong and weak ties from Marc Granovetter; chains of finance from Diane-Laure Arjaliès et al.; communities of practice from Davida Nicolini et al.; and incumbent groups versus challenger groups from Neil Fligstein and Doug McAdam. These concepts are all well established in social science, but we have combined and synthesized them here in a way that helps to explain why financial intermediaries behave as they do and why this behavior, while not always seemingly rational in an economic sense, is tolerated by other actors in the field.

After looking at two key groups of actors in the investment field—buy-side fund management teams and sell-side equity research analysts—in terms of how they interact with one another and how they combine to defend their collective interests and field position, we offer a view of financial markets as constituted by slowly evolving communities whose habits, routines, and epistemologies can be difficult to shift, even when faced with overwhelming evidence that what they are doing doesn't work most of the time. This is quite different from a behavioral approach to understanding financial intermediaries, which focuses on cognitive biases held at the individual level.[16] We take issue with the behavioral approach because it ignores the importance of social structures to the shaping of economic action.

Our community-centered view of financial markets is also distinct from many well-established economic sociology approaches to understanding financial intermediaries. Often economic sociology privileges the interactions between material infrastructures and nonhuman objects.[17] Sociologically we have no issue with an actor-network theory (ANT) approach per se. We recognize that it has offered a wealth of new insights into how action in financial markets is increasingly interspersed with technological change. It has an undoubted capacity to explain modern phenomena such as computer-mediated flash crashes. Indeed, we have sought to approach this book with a socio-technical sensitivity, which is evident from the attention we have paid to customer relationship management systems and the way in which consensus numbers are produced via ubiquitous information devices such as Bloomberg terminals.

There are limits to and problems with a full-blown ANT perspective, however. Exponents of ANT often fixate on the sharp end of technological change. This leads us into danger-ous territory, whereby images of financial markets as innova-tive, dynamic, and disruptive are conjured up. We certainly accept that it is important to highlight areas of change and that technology is reshaping many aspects of social and eco-nomic life. However, such a perspective potentially lends itself to co-option by certain economic schools of thought that see market forces as benign and inexorable forces that cannot, and should not, be tamed. ANT micro insights can lead to myopia if not complemented by broader issues of political economy. In other words, the socio-technical systems that comprise financial markets are not of sufficient interest in and of themselves. We also need to think about hierarchies, concentrations of power, decisions by elites, and the effects on society.

In contrast, our field perspective advanced here emphasizes the defensiveness, habits, and purposeful inertia of different communities, highlighting how financial markets are socially constructed. Moreover, as difficult as it is to dislodge incum-bents from their field positions, such a conceptualization readily reminds us that financial markets are not, *pace* ANT, ontolog-ically flat entities but complex social structures that produce winners and losers. Our community view asserts that financial markets can be constructed differently, should the political will to do so exist. Ultimately markets need not be uncontrollable juggernauts or all-powerful leviathans; they are made by people and consequently can be remade by people.

THE FUTURE OF THE INVESTMENT FIELD

It is tempting to view the active fund management community as a population on the verge of collapse, its members diminishing in numbers as the ecosystem surrounding them becomes less and less bountiful. However, we believe that would be a rational fallacy on our part. History is full of bad or outdated ideas that manage to persist despite their shortcomings having been well recognized—from the QWERTY keyboard,[18] to fossil-fuel addiction,[19] to religious cults[20] and beyond. Active fund management, irrespective of its epistemological legitimacy, may well persist due to the purposeful action of its member groups. The current trend in financial markets indicates there will be less active and more passive investment going forward,[21] but that does not mean that the one will fully replace the other. As long as financial markets exist more or less in their present form, some groups will always attempt to outperform others and will claim that alpha generation is possible on a consistent basis. That being said, it is worth stressing that many of our respondents saw a diminished role for the active community in the future, which is possibly more a harbinger of the future composition of financial markets than are the views of those respondents who were more bullish about the active community's future relevance.

This points toward a changing of the epistemic guard going forward, with the heterodox challenger group, the passive community, quickly becoming a dominant player in the investment field. With its newfound dominance will come a newly established orthodoxy in the form of an epistemic regime that privileges a habitus that is replicative rather than hypothesis driven. While it is hard to lament the demise of active fund management, given the wealth it has effectively extracted from society over the last century and a half,[22] it is not entirely clear that the material arrangements that would follow from a world built around passive investment would produce better social outcomes. In the immediate term, it seems hard to dispute that index investing offers better returns for those whose futures are tied up in pension funds and other investment vehicles. However, in the new asset manager capitalism, one of the objectives pursued is the maximization of assets under management.[23] This has led to a concentration of assets such that Vanguard is now the top owner of over half of the companies in the S&P 500, and the big two indexers, Vanguard and Blackrock, are among the top three holdings of 90 percent of the S&P 500.[24] Oligopolies rarely produce good social outcomes.

Irrespective of the increasingly oligopolistic nature of index investing, an investment world dominated by passive investing may well have problematic consequences for corporate governance.[25] Even if we dismiss the rather hopeful arguments around environmental, social, and governance investing that active community members espouse in the course of defending their own field position, we must recognize that the philosophy of index investing is built around investment returns rather than social welfare; it privileges asset owners rather than society per se. This is sometimes forgotten in the debate over whether active or passive investors will place greater pressure on corporate management to behave better. Neither is well suited for this role, and their economic incentives make it less likely that they will place environmental or social aspects above economic criteria.

If society wants organizations to behave differently, it should look not to the asset management industry but to policy makers to enact these changes. This is not to say that financial markets hold no power. On the contrary, they hold more power than companies do, the latter being the playthings of the former.[26] Rather, it is to say that if we want to live in a world that produces very different social and environmental outcomes, then financial markets and ownership structures must be reformed in ways that go beyond simply replacing one dominant group of asset managers with another.

FUTURE RESEARCH DIRECTIONS

The key conceptual markers laid out in this book—a community-centered understanding of financial fields, purposeful inertia, and epistemic and social structures—could be used in future research studies to develop a fuller understanding of financial intermediaries and the way they structure financial markets. Effectively these concepts could travel up and down the chain of finance[27] and be used to interrogate the field positions, epistemologies, and social dynamics of various groups of financial intermediaries.

In this regard, one crucial question that, as far as we are aware, has yet to be explored in any detail by social science disciplines is why so much money still flows into active fund management even though the economic analysis appears to suggest that better outcomes are offered elsewhere. We can speculate about the purposeful inertia that might be prevalent in the ecosystem surrounding active fund management. For example, many of the assets flowing into fund management do not come from individuals but from other financial institutions such as pension funds, insurance companies, other fund management companies (a curious, seemingly pointless additional link in the chain of finance), and a legion of wealth management and investment advice companies that funnel individual investments toward larger institutional players. What congealed social relations and ossified epistemic regimes are prevalent in these different subspaces within the investment field? Are the economic incentives to channel money toward active funds superior to those to channel money toward passive funds? What evidence is there of purposeful inertia among pension fund trustees, wealth managers, investment advisers, etc.? We know relatively little about such groups,[28] but these are important questions to answer, both to advance our understanding of the social and epistemic underpinnings of financial markets and to potentially identify better economic outcomes for society.

A further area of enquiry worthy of exploration in more detail is the passive investment community. Although a key construct in the current book, the passive community has featured obliquely as a prop (albeit one that was offered up unprompted by our respondents) used to elucidate the beliefs and epistemic attachments of the active investment community. We have a good sense of the passive community's epistemic regime from published material, but beyond quantitative studies that document the investment performance of passive versus active funds[29] and a few more-journalistic accounts of index fund pioneers,[30] we know little about how the passive investment community is structured in terms of interpersonal ties and interinstitutional dependencies. One pilot interview that we conducted as part of a nascent foray into this domain suggested that the chain of financial intermediation is no less complicated for passive investing than it is for active investing. We therefore suspect that the opportunity for congealed social relations is still there, although this might be mitigated by the extent to which passive investment decisions rely less on the rich narratives that emanate from interpersonal interactions. These hypotheses may be well founded or not. Their testing is a matter for empirical research.

Additionally, we have been rather binary in our presentation of the investment field as made up of two relatively distinct communities of practice. This is reflective of how the players of the investment game speak about one another and themselves, and we have followed this discursive binary. However, probing beneath the discourse of active versus passive investing reveals more heterogeneous groupings of investment players. For example, many exchange-traded funds (ETFs) are now thematic in orientation. They may focus on tech stocks or exclude companies that are involved in arms manufacture. One ETF has even been set up to make trades that are the exact opposite of recommendations by Jim Cramer from CNBC's *Mad Money*.

Applying such criteria effectively adds an extra decision-making layer onto the ETF ownership structure, pushing these funds in the direction of active management. Similarly, some active managers might follow strategies that are very similar to those used by index funds. Some of our respondents used the phrase "enhanced index" to describe what they did and "passive plus" to denote more-quantitative/systematic strategies that identify key investment factors (e.g., growth or market capitalization) that end up keeping the investment fund's performance very close to that of an index. Those who use such strategies are often pejoratively labeled "index huggers" by those possessing a more hypothesis-driven habitus.[31] Also, *smart beta* is a term widely used to describe what are, in effect, index strategies with a bit of active interference added into them.

This all suggests that there is more of a spectrum than a binary or, alternatively, that many players of the investment game occupy a liminal space between the active and passive communities. Future research could explore in more detail this spectrum and chart the different financial epistemologies that prevail in each group, along with the social relations that congeal around them.

METHODOLOGICAL APPENDIX

SPEAKING TO THE PROPHETS OF ALPHA

AS WE alluded to at various junctures in this book, there was something serendipitous about how we arrived at our focus on the active fund management community and its social and epistemic structures. Initially we were motivated by a narrower set of intellectual concerns that centered around changing interactions between those working in fund management (buy-side) and the equity research analysts (sell-side), whom they hire seemingly to provide input into their investment decisions. As academics working in the accounting and finance departments of business schools, we were curious why the vast literature on equity analysts ignored how they interacted with their paymasters on the buy-side and focused instead on the published research outputs of analysts such as responses to quarterly earnings updates, price targets, and earnings forecasts.

Sociologically such an approach completely erases the social and cultural context surrounding economic actors, which we found intellectually implausible. Add to this the concerns of an ex-practitioner in the field—who returned to academia after a successful career as an equity analyst at Morgan Stanley (Author C)—that extant academic research fails to describe what equity analysts actually do in a plausible fashion, and we felt that we had a potentially interesting research project. Specifically our intention was to look at the social and cultural context surrounding equity analysts, which we could do by exploring their interactions with other economic actors in the field as we sought to better understand what value they brought (if any) to the investment decisions of their fund management clients.

WHAT DID WE WANT TO EXPLORE?

In order to proceed, we constructed a qualitative research design that would engage buy-side and sell-side actors directly.[1] The value of a qualitative approach, which deals with real-life financial intermediaries rather than their published outputs (as in quantitative approaches) or their proxies (as in experiments that often enlist MBA students who don't even work in finance), is that it elicits narratives about what actually happens in practice. The questions we were interested in asking included these:

- For what does the buy-side value the sell-side?
- Could the buy-side operate with less input from the sell-side?
- Are there too many analysts working in the investment field?

- What is the key to success as a sell-side analyst?
- What technological changes are evident in the field?
- As a sell-side analyst, how do you allocate your time to research, site visits, marketing, non-deal road shows, or other activities?
- What major secular changes are taking place in the investment field?

We chose interviews over other methods such as ethnography and participant observation, as this would allow us breadth and permit us to draw greater generalizations from the study[2] and would lend itself to what was always intended to be a trans-Atlantic study involving more than one research site.

WHO DID WE SPEAK TO AND WHY?

Potential research participants were identified from a private database of investment professionals administered by a training company focused on equity research analysts and from personal contacts in Chicago, New York, and London. We chose these cities because they are major financial centers that house a range of buy-side and sell-side firms and also because we were variously acquainted with the financial landscape from either having worked there as a practitioner (Author C: London, New York, and Chicago) or having used these cities as sites of previous research studies (Author A: Chicago and London; Author B: London). By splitting sampling between the UK and the United States, we were also afforded the opportunity to both compare any differences between the two locations, thereby highlighting institutional variation, and to identify more global trends in the investment field.

We collected data sequentially, first in Chicago (April 2019, N = 20), then in New York (June 2019, N = 12), and finally in London (July 2019, N = 24). We also undertook a number of interviews via Zoom in 2021 to explore emerging themes, both with individuals we had previously interviewed and with new respondents. In total, between 2019 and 2021 we undertook seventy interviews, split among the three locations and between buy-side and sell-side actors. Table A.1 shows the interviewees'

TABLE A.1 Interviewees

Interviewee	Location	Date	Buy-side (BS)/ sell-side (SS)	Pseudonym for book
1	Chicago	April 2019	SS	Nathan
2	Chicago	April 2019	BS (formerly SS)	George
3	Chicago	April 2019	BS	Murray
4	Chicago	April 2019	BS (formerly SS)	Derek
5	Chicago	April 2019	BS	Chris
6	Chicago	April 2019	BS	Dylan
7	Chicago	April 2019	BS	Amal
8	Chicago	April 2019	BS (formerly SS)	Jingqi
9	Chicago	April 2019	BS (formerly SS)	Reuben
10	Chicago	April 2019	BS	Alan
11	Chicago	April 2019	BS	Crispin
12	Chicago	April 2019	SS	Danny
13	Chicago	April 2019	BS	Maynard

14	Chicago	April 2019	SS	James
15	Chicago	April 2019	SS	Pierce
16	Chicago	April 2019	BS	Kevin
17	Chicago	April 2019	BS	Louis
18	Chicago	April 2019	SS	Ethan
19	Chicago	April 2019	BS	Steve
20	Chicago	April 2019	BS	Mahesh
21	New York City	June 2019	SS	Christian
22	New York City	June 2019	SS	Drew
23	New York City	June 2019	SS	Shaun
24	New York City	June 2019	BS	Vaughan
25	New York City	June 2019	SS (formerly BS)	Ivan
26	New York City	June 2019	SS	Nish
27	New York City	June 2019	SS	Nico
28	New York City	June 2019	SS	Jae
29	New York City	June 2019	SS	Eric
30	New York City	June 2019	BS	Karl
31	New York City	June 2019	BS	Carlos
32	New York City	June 2019	SS	Ray
33	London	July 2019	SS	Clara
34	London	July 2019	BS	Felix
35	London	July 2019	BS	Jasper
36	London	July 2019	BS	Guido
37	London	July 2019	SS (formerly BS)	Salim
38	London	July 2019	SS	Albert
39	London	July 2019	BS (quant	Will
40	London	July 2019	SS (formerly BS)—paid by corporate clients for coverage	Geoff
41	London	July 2019	BS (formerly SS/ independent research)	Grant
42	London	July 2019	BS	Heman
43	London	July 2019	BS	Terence
44	London	July 2019	BS	Melvyn

(*Continued*)

Interviewee	Location	Date	Buy-side (BS)/ sell-side (SS)	Pseudonym for book
45	London	July 2019	SS	Lucia
46	London	July 2019	SS	Alice
47	London	July 2019	BS (formerly SS)	Karen
48	London	July 2019	SS	Tom
49	London	July 2019	BS (quant)	Harold
50	London	July 2019	SS	Michel
51	London	August 2019	SS	Ashley
52	London	July 2019	BS (fixed income)	François
53	London	April 2019	SS (quant)	Alex
54	London	May 2019	SS (formerly BS; specialist in valuing illiquid assets)	Kristoff
55	London (India-based)	April 2019	BS (formerly SS; macro)	Swapnesh
56	London (India-based)	April 2019	BS	Vijay
57	London	March 2021	BS (formerly SS/ independent research)	Martha
58	London	March 2021	BS	Andrew
59	London	March 2021	SS	Jamie
60	London	March 2021	SS	Phillip
61	London	March 2021	SS	Joel
62	London	March 2021	BS	Grant
63	London	March 2021	BS	Angus
64	London	March 2021	BS	Charles
65	London	March 2021	BS	Ahmed
66	London	March 2021	SS	Jaymal
67	London	March 2021	BS	Guanming
68	London	April 2021	FJ (financial journalist)	Raymond
69	London	April 2021	BS	Gustav
70	London	May 2021	BS	Tim

characteristics, including physical location, month of interview, position in the field (i.e., buy-side or sell-side), and pseudonym for the purposes of this book.

In total, we spoke to twenty-eight sell-side actors and forty-two buy-side actors, which appears to be a slightly skewed sample, although we deliberately privileged buy-side actors slightly more than sell-side actors in our sampling because the practices and professional worldviews implied by our theoretical framework were likely to be more evident in cross-role interactions in the field and potentially present the sell-side in a less than flattering light. As such, we were keen to determine, in addition to how the sell-side sees itself, how the sell-side is perceived by the buy-side. This proviso notwithstanding, it should be borne in mind that twelve of our participants had worked on both the buy-side and the sell-side during their careers, and they were in a position to comment more holistically on buy-side/sell-side interactions.

There is no ideal number of interview participants in qualitative research, although a survey of 798 qualitative workplace/organization studies showed a norm of 15–60 participants and a median of 32.5 interviewees, which we have significantly exceeded here.[3] Another key guide for participant recruitment is theoretical saturation, the point at which new interviews stop revealing substantively new themes and sufficient material has been accumulated to answer the study's research questions.[4] We felt that we achieved such saturation with our own study, particularly after having conducted an additional fourteen interviews in 2021.

Our seventy interviews captured a broad spectrum of different investment professionals, measured by different relevant factors such as tenure, size of firm, and investment strategies. For example, on the buy-side, our participants were involved with assets under management ranging from just over $120 million up to $135 billion, with the average being $14 billion. Their experience and seniority ranged from one year out of college to thirty years in the fund management industry. On the sell-side, our participants were drawn from a range of analyst firms, including specialist research providers, boutique investment houses, and bulge-bracket investment banks. Again, the experience of our sell-side participants ranged considerably, from two years out of college to twenty years in the field. We also tried to find interviewees who had a range of investable universes. An investable universe refers to the parameters that an asset manager places around their fund and may include, for example, all U.S. mid-cap equities, European large-cap pharmaceuticals, or global technology stocks. The investable universes of our interviewees covered various sectors, including technology, financial services, real estate, industrials, and transportation. While all of the sell-side analysts and most of the buy-side analysts were assigned to specific industries, some in the buy-side population were generalists, in that they focused on any industry of interest, although they may have had geography- or size-related parameters that limited their universe. The vast majority of interviewees were male ($N = 53$), which is largely reflective of the gender composition of the equity analyst and fund management communities.[5]

The majority of the interviews took place at either university premises (Chicago) or specific office space rented for the purposes of the study (London and New York), with approximately fifteen interviews also undertaken at the participant's place of work. The twelve follow-up interviews completed in early 2021 were undertaken via Zoom due to Covid-19 restrictions in place at the time. All of the interviews were recorded and subsequently transcribed, with the exception of three for which the interviewees preferred not to be recorded. In those cases, extensive notes were taken, and these were subsequently interrogated following the same data analysis techniques used for the interview transcripts.

The interviews were sixty to ninety minutes in length. The initial interview protocol was designed to explore the themes identified previously. In response to the last theme—secular changes evident in the field—initial interviews in Chicago identified passive investing as a major disruptive force in asset management. As such, this became an explicit theme that we then raised with interviewees in subsequent rounds of data collection in New York and London.

HOW DID WE MAKE SENSE OF WHAT OUR RESPONDENTS TOLD US?

Having transcribed all of the audio recordings from our interviews, we undertook several rounds of substantive coding of the data using NVivo qualitative data software. Our process was shaped by various methodological and conceptual parameters. In practical terms, the coding followed an iterative process that first privileged descriptive codes, which were then progressively grouped into more abstract, theoretical categories.[6]

Conceptually, as this coding process took place, we used our various theoretical inspirations as ideas that were "good to think with,"[7] meaning that we didn't seek to slavishly apply these ideas so much as we used these theories to help direct us toward patterns in the data that we might build upon and elaborate ourselves. As much as we can be explicit about this— and it should be stressed that theorizing about qualitative data is a process that is not always transparent, even to those who are doing the theorizing[8]—we started to identify how actors constructed meaning about their social environment[9] and also seemingly internalized the surrounding rules of the active investment game.[10] Throughout this process, we kept in mind the injunction from relational sociology to remain sensitive to the dynamics of interactions, which are arguably the most important unit of analysis for the scientific study of social life.[11]

All members of the writing team read the transcripts and then discussed them during regular data analysis meetings. This inductive process served to identify a number of first-order codes, which were then read and discussed by all members of the "interpretive community" in order to establish coder reliability.[12] These discussions identified a number of overlaps and higher-level themes into which the first-order codes were collapsed. As a result of these discussions, we identified larger, aggregate categories, which fed into the second-order data analysis. This involved iterative reviews of the data, relevant literature, and social theory. We looked at overlapping themes and relabeled certain first-order categories accordingly. A limited number of interview quotes were coded more than once, as they resonated with more than one identified theme. The move from first- to second- to eventually third-order codes did not proceed until all authors were happy with interpretations at each transition stage, following methodological best practice.[13]

Zooming out from the nuts and bolts of data coding, we were always careful to adopt a sociology of our own sociology,[14] recognizing our own potential complicity in creating the world that we seek to describe.[15] In practical terms, this meant we had to be attuned to the various struggles inherent to the investment field that we were analyzing rather than inadvertently simply offering our own opinions of that field's actors, its overall social consequences, etc. In other words, we needed to describe, as much as possible, the research object (the investment field) rather than our relation to it (our envy, excitement, distaste, curiosity, etc.). This is a particular challenge when researchers are embedded in some way in the field itself,[16] as one member of the writing team was (previously as an equity analyst but also as an ongoing consultant to equity research teams). This embeddedness posed a challenge for data analysis, as we had to ensure sufficient distance between conceptual concerns and the lived experiences of our research subjects. We addressed this issue by assigning this member of the research team the role of critical observer during the data analysis phase, involved in but not leading the coding process. Embeddedness also presented an opportunity for both data collection and data analysis in the sense that reading between the lines of respondents' declarations was possible, as was identifying key omissions from the narratives of some interviewees. Overall, this helped the research team to more effectively compare and contrast the statements of different respondents.

NOTES

INTRODUCTION

1. James Chen, "Financial Intermediary: What It Means, How It Works, Examples," Investopedia, updated September 23, 2020, https://www.investopedia.com/terms/f/financialintermediary.asp.
2. John Kenneth Galbraith, *The Affluent Society* (Houghton Mifflin Harcourt, 1998).
3. Madison Darbyshire, "Cathie Wood's Flagship Ark Fund Tops $300mn in Fees Despite Losses," *Financial Times*, March 9, 2023, https://www.ft.com/content/7930fbf7-d2d6-464c-9ffa-20efcf58e21e; Rupert Neate, "Fall of Neil Woodford Puts Future of Fund Management Under Scrutiny," *The Guardian*, October 19, 2019, https://www.theguardian.com/business/2019/oct/19/neil-woodford-demise-puts-fund-management-industry-under-scrutiny.
4. Hendrik Bessembinder, Michael J. Cooper, and Feng Zhang, "Mutual Fund Performance at Long Horizons," *Journal of Financial Economics* 147, no. 1 (2023), 132.
5. Theodore Sougiannis and Takashi Yaekura, "The Accuracy and Bias of Equity Values Inferred from Analysts' Earnings Forecasts," *Journal of Accounting, Auditing & Finance* 16, no. 4 (2001): 331–362.

6. Diane-Laure Arjaliès, Philip Grant, Iain Hardie, Donald MacKenzie, and Ekaterina Svetlova, *Chains of Finance: How Investment Management Is Shaped* (Oxford: Oxford University Press, 2019).

7. Eric Balchunas, *The Bogle Effect: How John Bogle and Vanguard Turned Wall Street Inside Out and Saved Investors Trillions* (Dallas: BenBella Books, 2022).

8. Davide Nicolini, Igor Pyrko, Omid Omidvar, and Agnessa Spanellis, "Understanding Communities of Practice: Taking Stock and Moving Forward," *Academy of Management Annals* 16, no. 2 (2022): 680–718.

9. Robert Seyfert, "Bugs, Predations or Manipulations? Incompatible Epistemic Regimes of High-Frequency Trading," *Economy and Society* 45, no. 2 (2016): 251–277.

10. Marc S. Granovetter, "The Strength of Weak Ties," *American Journal of Sociology* 78, no. 6 (1973): 1360–1380.

11. Richard Sennett, *The Craftsman* (New Haven, CT: Yale University Press, 2009).

12. Pierre Bourdieu, *The Field of Cultural Production* (New York: Columbia University Press, 1993).

13. One of the few studies to use Bourdieu's theory in the context of active fund management is John Millar, "The Gilded Path: Capital, Habitus and Illusio in the Fund Management Field," *Accounting, Auditing & Accountability Journal* 34, no. 8 (2021): 1906–1931.

14. Will Leggett, "The Politics of Behaviour Change: Nudge, Neoliberalism and the State," *Policy & Politics* 42, no. 1 (2014): 3–19.

15. Bob Jessop, "Capitalist Diversity and Variety: Variegation, the World Market, Compossibility and Ecological Dominance," *Capital & Class* 38, no. 1 (2014): 45–58.

16. Michael B. Clement and Sunyo T. Tse, "Financial Analyst Characteristics and Herding Behavior in Forecasting," *Journal of Finance* 60, no. 1 (2005): 307–341.

17. Kathryn Kadous, Molly Mercer, and Jane Thayer, "Is There Safety in Numbers? The Effects of Forecast Accuracy and Forecast Boldness on Financial Analysts' Credibility with Investors," *Contemporary Accounting Research* 26, no. 3 (2010): 933–968.

18. Nicolini et al., "Understanding Communities of Practice."

19. Alex Preda, *Noise: Living and Trading in Electronic Finance* (Chicago: University of Chicago Press, 2017).

1. FINANCIAL INTERMEDIARIES

1. Diane-Laure Arjaliès, Philip Grant, Iain Hardie, Donald A. MacKenzie, and Ekaterina Svetlova, *Chains of Finance: How Investment Management Is Shaped* (Oxford: Oxford University Press, 2017).

2. It should be noted that there is an increasing tendency for asset allocators to circumvent public markets and to invest in companies directly. While we do not explore that tendency in this book, a recent analysis is offered by Brett Christophers, *Our Lives in Their Portfolios: Why Asset Managers Own the World* (London: Verso Books, 2023). In principle, this would suggest that some financial disintermediation is taking place in such a scenario, but it may be equally plausible that the intermediation has simply gone in-house as pension funds and other asset allocators expand their own internal investment management teams.

3. City of London and HM Treasury, *State of the Sector: Annual Review of UK Financial Services 2023* (London: City of London and HM Treasury, 2023), https://assets.publishing.service.gov.uk/media/64ad6d32fe36e0000d-6fa6a9/State_of_the_sector_annual_review_of_UK_financial_services _2023.pdf.

4. Thomas Philippon, "Has the US Finance Industry Become Less Efficient? On the Theory and Measurement of Financial Intermediation," *American Economic Review* 105, no. 4 (2005): 1408–1438.

5. Jeremy Greenwood and Boyan Jovanovic, "Financial Development, Growth, and the Distribution of Income," *Journal of Political Economy* 98, no. 5, pt. 1 (1990): 1076–1107.

6. Investment Company Institute, *2023 Investment Company Fact Book* (Washington, DC: Investment Company Institute, 2023), 48, https://www.ici.org/system/files/2023-05/2023-factbook.pdf.pdf.

7. Morningstar, "Morningstar's US Active/Passive Barometer: Year-End 2023," https://www.morningstar.com/lp/active-passive-barometer.

8. Ed Moisson, *The Economics of Fund Management* (Newcastle Upon Tyne, UK: Agenda, 2022).

9. See James J. Valentine, *Best Practices for Equity Research Analysts: Essentials for Buy-Side and Sell-Side Analysts* (New York: McGraw-Hill Education, 2011), for an overview.

10. Shahed Imam and Crawford Spence, "Context, Not Predictions: A Field Study of Financial Analysts," *Accounting, Auditing & Accountability*

Journal 29, no. 2 (2016): 226–247; Yuval Millo, Crawford Spence, and James J. Valentine, "The Field of Investment Advice: The Social Forces That Govern Equity Analysts," *Accounting Review* 98, no. 7 (2023): 457–477.

11. Lawrence D. Brown, Andrew C. Call, Michael B. Clement, and Nathan Y. Sharp, "The Activities of Buy-Side Analysts and the Determinants of Their Stock Recommendations," *Journal of Accounting and Economics* 62, no. 1 (2016): 139–156.

2. THE SOCIAL STRUCTURES OF FINANCIAL MARKETS

The epigraph to chapter 2 comes from Marc Granovetter, "Economic Institutions as Social Constructions: A Framework for Analysis," *Acta Sociologica* 35 (1992): 5.

1. See Sundaresh Ramnath, Steve Rock, and Philip B. Shane, "Financial Analysts' Forecasts and Stock Recommendations: A Review of the Research," *Foundations and Trends in Finance* 2, no. 4 (2008): 311–421, for a review of this literature. A more recent review was undertaken by Mark Bradshaw at al. in 2017 (see note 4), but this 2008 article remains among the most comprehensive to focus on analyst forecasts and stock recommendations, which is what interests the vast majority of the researchers.

2. Lawrence D. Brown, Andrew C. Call, Michael B. Clement, and Nathan Y. Sharp, "The Activities of Buy-Side Analysts and the Determinants of Their Stock Recommendations," *Journal of Accounting and Economics* 62, no. 1 (2016): 139–156.

3. Pierre Bourdieu, "The Scholastic Point of View," *Cultural Anthropology* 5, no. 4 (1992): 381.

4. See Mark Bradshaw, Yonca Ertimur, and Patricia O'Brien, "Financial Analysts and Their Contribution to Well-Functioning Capital Markets," *Foundations and Trends in Accounting* 11, no. 3 (2017): 119–191.

5. Fischer Black, "Noise," *Journal of Finance* 41, no. 3 (1986): 528–543. See also Alex Preda, *Noise: Living and Trading in Electronic Finance* (Chicago: University of Chicago Press, 2017), for a more critical discussion of the concept.

6. Bin Ke and Yong Yu, "The Effect of Issuing Biased Earnings Forecasts on Analysts' Access to Management and Survival," *Journal of Accounting Research* 44, no. 5 (2006): 965–999.

7. Pervin K. Shroff, Ramgopal Venkataraman, and Baohu Xin, "Timeliness of Analysts' Forecasts: The Information Content of Delayed Forecasts," *Contemporary Accounting Research* 31, no. 1 (2014): 202–229.

8. Jack Hirshleifer, "The Expanding Domain of Economics," *American Economic Review* 85 (1985), 53.

9. Diane-Laure Arjaliès, Philip Grant, Iain Hardie, Donald A. MacKenzie, and Ekaterina Svetlova, *Chains of Finance: How Investment Management Is Shaped* (Oxford: Oxford University Press, 2017).

10. See, for example, Eben Otuteye and Mohammad Siddiquee, "Underperformance of Actively Managed Portfolios: Some Behavioral Insights," *Journal of Behavioral Finance* 21, no. 3 (2020): 284–300.

11. See, for example, Tiana Lehmer, Ben Lourie, and Devin Shanthikumar, "Brokerage Trading Volume and Analysts' Earnings Forecasts: A Conflict of Interest?," *Review of Accounting Studies* 27, no. 2 (2022): 441–476.

12. A useful article on this topic is M. Rahman Jahidur, Jinxin Zhang, and Siwei Dong, "Factors Affecting the Accuracy of Analysts' Forecasts: A Review of the Literature," *Academy of Accounting and Financial Studies Journal* 23, no. 3 (2019): 1–18.

13. Amos Tversky and Daniel Kahneman, "Judgment Under Uncertainty: Heuristics and Biases: Biases in Judgments Reveal Some Heuristics of Thinking Under Uncertainty," *Science* 185, no. 4157 (1974): 1124–1131.

14. David Hirshleifer, "Behavioral Finance," *Annual Review of Economics* 7 (2015): 133–159.

15. Mary S. Morgan, "Economic Man as Model Man: Ideal Types, Idealization and Caricatures," *Journal of the History of Economic Thought* 8, no. 1 (2006): 1–27.

16. Kimberley Chong and David Tuckett, "Constructing Conviction Through Action and Narrative: How Money Managers Manage Uncertainty and the Consequence for Financial Market Functioning," *Socio-economic Review* 13, no. 2 (2015): 309–330.

17. See, for example, Vibha Gaba, Sunkee Lee, Phillip Meyer-Doyle, and Amy Zhao-Ding, "Prior Experience of Managers and Maladaptive Responses to Performance Feedback: Evidence from Mutual Funds," *Organization Science* 34, no. 2 (2023): 894–915.

18. David Hirshleifer, "Presidential Address: Social Transmission Bias in Economics and Finance," *Journal of Finance* 75, no. 4 (2020): 1779–1831.

19. Hirshleifer, "Behavioral Finance, 44"

20. Hirshleifer, "Presidential Address," 1817.

21. Hirshleifer, "Presidential Address."
22. Pierre Bourdieu, *The Social Structures of the Economy* (Cambridge: Polity Press, 2005), 198.
23. Bourdieu, *The Social Structures*, 197.
24. Adam S. Hayes, "The Behavioral Economics of Pierre Bourdieu," *Sociological Theory* 38, no. 1 (2020): 16–35.
25. Brooke Harrington, "Habitus and the Labor of Representation Among Elite Professionals," *Journal of Professions and Organization* 4, no. 3 (2017): 282–301.
26. Chris Carter and Crawford Spence, "Being a Successful Professional: An Exploration of Who Makes Partner in the Big Four," *Contemporary Accounting Research* 31, no. 4 (2014): 949–981.
27. Crawford Spence, Jingqi Zhu, Takahiro Endo, and Saori Matsubara, "Money, Honour and Duty: Global Professional Service Firms in Comparative Perspective," *Accounting, Organizations and Society* 62 (2017): 82–97.
28. Olivier Godechot, "Back in the Bazaar: Taking Pierre Bourdieu to a Trading Room," *Journal of Cultural Economy* 9, no. 4 (2016): 410–429.
29. John Millar, "The Gilded Path: Capital, Habitus and Illusio in the Fund Management Field," *Accounting, Auditing & Accountability Journal* 34, no. 8 (2021): 1906–1931.
30. Marc Granovetter, "Economic Action and Social Structure: The Problem of Embeddedness," *American Journal of Sociology* 91, no. 3 (1985): 487.
31. Granovetter, "Economic Action." See also Marc Granovetter, *Society and Economy: Framework and Principles* (Cambridge, MA: Belknap Press of Harvard University Press, 2017), 14.
32. Granovetter, "Economic Institutions," 8.
33. Mahdi Kafaee, Elade Daviran, and Mostafa Taqavi, "The QWERTY Keyboard from the Perspective of the Collingridge Dilemma: Lessons for Co-construction of Human-Technology," *AI & Society* (2022): 1–13.
34. Kafaee et al., "The QWERTY Keyboard," 9.
35. Fabian Muniesa, Yuval Millo, and Michel Callon, "An Introduction to Market Devices," *Sociological Review* 55, no. 2 supp. (2007): 1–12.
36. Donald MacKenzie, "Material Signals: A Historical Sociology of High-Frequency Trading," *American Journal of Sociology* 123, no. 6 (2018): 1635–1683.
37. Juan-Pablo Pardo-Guerra, *Automating Finance: Infrastructures, Engineers, and the Making of Electronic Markets* (Cambridge: Cambridge University Press, 2019).

38. Daniel Beunza, *Taking the Floor: Models, Morals, and Management in a Wall Street Trading Room* (Princeton, NJ: Princeton University Press, 2019).
39. Pierre Bourdieu, *Science de la Science et Réflexivité* (Paris: Raisons d'Agir, 2001).
40. Donald MacKenzie, *Trading at the Speed of Light: How Ultrafast Algorithms Are Transforming Financial Markets* (Princeton, NJ: Princeton University Press, 2021).
41. Pardo-Guerra, *Automating Finance.*
42. Bo Hee Min and Christian Borch, "Systemic Failures and Organizational Risk Management in Algorithmic Trading: Normal Accidents and High Reliability in Financial Markets," *Social Studies of Science* 52, no. 2 (2021): 277–302.
43. Dave Elder-Vass, "Searching for Realism, Structure and Agency in Actor Network Theory," *British Journal of Sociology* 59, no. 3 (2008): 455–473.
44. For a welcome, if rare, attempt to fuse political economy with ANT, see Donald Mackenzie and Alice Bamford, "Counterperformativity," *New Left Review* 113 (2018): 97–121.
45. Bourdieu, "The Scholastic Point of View."
46. Charles Camic, "Bourdieu's Cleft Sociology of Science," *Minerva* 49 (2011): 275–293.
47. Pierre Bourdieu, *The Field of Cultural Production* (New York: Columbia University Press, 1993), 163.
48. Pierre Bourdieu, "The Specificity of the Scientific Field: The Social Conditions of the Progress of Reason," *Social Science Information* 14 (1975): 29.
49. Pierre Bourdieu and Loïc Wacquant, *An Invitation to Reflexive Sociology* (Cambridge: Polity Press, 1992).
50. The following articles provide in-depth discussion of the epistemic bounds of different expert groups, with Seyfert, in particular, elaborating the concept of epistemic regime (which will be discussed further in chapters 6 and 7): Len Seabrooke and Eleni Tsingou, "Distinctions, Affiliations, and Professional Knowledge in Financial Reform Expert Groups," *Journal of European Public Policy* 21, no. 3 (2014): 389–407; and Robert Seyfert, "Bugs, Predations or Manipulations? Incompatible Epistemic Regimes of High-Frequency Trading," *Economy and Society* 45, no. 2 (2016): 251–277.
51. Donald MacKenzie, "Mechanizing the Merc: The Chicago Mercantile Exchange and the Rise of High-Frequency Trading," *Technology and Culture* 56, no. 3 (2015): 646–675.

52. Godechot, "Back in the Bazaar."
53. Alex Preda, "Where Do Analysts Come From? The Case of Financial Chartism," *Sociological Review* 55, no. 2 supp. (2007): 40–64.
54. Daniel Beunza and David Stark, "How to Recognize Opportunities: Heterarchical Search in a Trading Room," in *The Sociology of Financial Markets*, ed. Karin Knorr Cetina and Alex Preda (Oxford: Oxford University Press, 2005), 84–101.
55. Daniel Beunza and Raghu Garud, "Calculators, Lemmings or Frame-Makers? The Intermediary Role of Securities Analysts," *Sociological Review* 55, no. 2 supp. (2007): 13–39.
56. See Scott James and Lucia Quaglia, "Epistemic Contestation and Interagency Conflict: The Challenge of Regulating Investment Funds," *Regulation and Governance* 17, no. 3 (2023): 346–362, which illustrates the epistemic differences between prudential and securities regulators in the context of shadow banking.
57. Davide Nicolini, Igor Pyrko, Omid Omidvar, and Agnessa Spanellis, "Understanding Communities of Practice: Taking Stock and Moving Forward," *Academy of Management Annals* 16, no. 2 (2022): 680–718.
58. Pierre Bourdieu, *Sociology in Question* (London: Sage, 2003), 73.
59. Neil Fligstein and Doug McAdam, *A Theory of Fields* (New York: Oxford University Press, 2012).
60. Fligstein and McAdam, *A Theory of Fields*, 3.

3. SOCIAL STICKINESS

The epigraphs to chapter 3 come from Durkheim, Emile (1964) *The Division of Labour in Society*, New York: The Free Press.; and Weber, M. (1978). Economy and Society, Ed. By Guenther Roth and Claus Witich, Berkeley (CA). Both the Durkheim and Weber quotes appear in Charles Camic's excellent article on habit: "The Matter of Habit," *American Journal of Sociology* 91, no. 5 (1986): 1051, 1058.
1. Erving Goffman, *The Presentation of Self in Everyday Life* (New York: Doubleday, 1959), 259.
2. Camic, "The Matter of Habit."
3. Pierre Bourdieu and Loïc Wacquant, *An Invitation to Reflexive Sociology* (Cambridge: Polity Press, 1992).
4. Pierre Bourdieu, *Outline of a Theory of Practice*, trans. Richard Nice (Cambridge: Cambridge University Press, 1977).

5. Bourdieu et seq., but for the specifically affective, corporeal, and cognitive triptych, see Loïc Wacquant, "Homines in Extremis: What Fighting Scholars Teach Us About Habitus," *Body & Society* 20, no. 2 (2014): 3–17.
6. Patricia M. Dechow, Amy P. Hutton, and Richard G. Sloan, "The Relation Between Analysts' Forecasts of Long-Term Earnings Growth and Stock Price Performance Following Equity Offerings," *Contemporary Accounting Research* 17, no. 1 (2000): 1–32.
7. Olaf Stotz and Rüdiger von Nitzsch, "The Perception of Control and the Level of Overconfidence: Evidence from Analyst Earnings Estimates and Price Targets," *Journal of Behavioral Finance* 6, no. 3 (2005): 121–128.
8. Barbara Barber, Reuven Lehavy, Maureen McNichols, and Brett Trueman, "Reassessing the Returns to Analysts' Stock Recommendations," *Financial Analysts Journal* 59, no. 2 (2003): 88–96.
9. Marc Granovetter, *Society and Economy: Framework and Principles* (Cambridge, MA: Belknap Press of Harvard University Press, 2017), 58.
10. Lauren A. Rivera, "Hiring as Cultural Matching: The Case of Elite Professional Service Firms," *American Sociological Review* 77, no. 6 (2012): 999–1022.
11. Josie Cox, "The Face of Wall Street Is Changing but Gender Inequality Runs Deep," *Forbes Magazine*, May 27, 2021, https://www.forbes.com/sites/josiecox/2021/05/27/the-face-of-wall-street-is-changing-but-gender-inequality-runs-deep/?sh=2b329a10443a.
12. Integrity Research Associates, "Corporate Access vs. Expert Networks—Any Difference?," December 13, 2010, https://www.integrity-research.com/corporate-access-vs-expert-networks---any-difference/.
13. EBITDA denotes earnings before interest, tax, depreciation, and amortization and is used by analysts, investors, and companies alike as a measure of the raw ability of a company to produce income.
14. K. Hung Chan, Ray R. Wang, and Ruixin Wang, "The Macbeth Factor: The Dark Side of Achievement-Driving Analysts," *Abacus* 57, no. 2 (2020): 325–361.
15. Christian Lo, Janne P. Breimo, and Hannu Turba, "Trust and Distrust in Interorganizational Networks—the Case of Norwegian Child Welfare and Protection," *Public Management Review* 24, no. 8 (2022): 1271–1288.
16. Giulio Anselmi and Giovanni Petrella, "Regulation and Stock Market Quality: The Impact of MiFID II Provision on Research Unbundling," *International Review of Financial Analysis* 76 (2021): art. 101788.

17. Gerard P. Hodgkinson, "Cognitive Inertia in a Turbulent Market: The Case of UK Residential Estate Agents," *Journal of Management Studies* 34, no. 6 (1997): 921–945.
18. Durkheim, *The Division of Labor.*
19. David A. Maber, Boris Groysberg, and Paul M. Healy, "An Empirical Examination of Sell-Side Brokerage Analysts' Published Research, Concierge Services, and High-Touch Services," *European Accounting Review* 30, no. 4 (2021): 827–853.
20. Adam S. Hayes, "The Behavioral Economics of Pierre Bourdieu," *Sociological Theory* 38, no. 1 (2020): 16–35.

4. CONFORMITY AND CONSENSUS

The epigraph to chapter 4 comes from Pierre Bourdieu, "La Fabrique des Débats Publics," *Le Monde Diplomatique,* January 2012.

1. Gonzalo Cortazar, Hector Ortega, and Consuelo Valencia, "How Good Are Analyst Forecasts of Oil Prices?," *Energy Economics* 102 (2021): art. 105500.
2. Sanghyuk Byun and Kirstin Roland, "Analyst Bias and Forecast Consistency," *Accounting & Finance* 61, no. 4 (2021): 5403–5437.
3. Adam S. Hayes, "The Behavioral Economics of Pierre Bourdieu," *Sociological Theory* 38, no. 1 (2020): 16–35.
4. Philip L. Baird, "Do Investors Recognize Biases in Securities Analysts' Forecasts?," *Review of Financial Economics* 38, no. 4 (2020): 623–634.
5. Robin Wigglesworth, "Bloomberg Is Contemplating Life Without Its Founder," *FT Magazine*, April 20, 2023.
6. Michel Callon, "Some Elements of a Sociology of Translation: Domestication of the Scallops and the Fishermen of St Brieuc Bay," *Sociological Review* 32, supp. 1 (1984): 196–233.
7. Pierre Bourdieu, *The Logic of Practice*, trans. Richard Nice (Stanford, CA: Stanford University Press, 1990), 66.
8. Itzhak Ben-David, Kiacui Li, Andrea Rossi, and Yang Song, "What Do Mutual Fund Investors Really Care About?," *Review of Financial Studies* 35, no. 4 (2022): 1723–1774.
9. K. C. Chan, "On the Contrarian Investment Strategy," *Journal of Business* 61, no. 2 (1988): 147–163.
10. Gus De Franco and Yibin Zhou, "The Performance of Analysts with a CFA Designation: The Role of Human-Capital and Signaling Theories," *Accounting Review* 84, no. 2 (2009): 383–404.

11. Richard Swedberg, "How to Use Max Weber's Ideal Type in Sociological Analysis," *Journal of Classical Sociology* 18, no. 3 (2018): 181–196.

12. Charles Camic, "Bourdieu's Cleft Sociology of Science," *Minerva* 49 (2011): 275–293.

13. Pierre Bourdieu, "The Specificity of the Scientific Field: The Social Conditions of the Progress of Reason," *Social Science Information* 14 (1979): 29.

14. David A. Maber, Boris Groysberg, and Paul M. Healy, "An Empirical Examination of Sell-Side Brokerage Analysts' Published Research, Concierge Services, and High-Touch Services," *European Accounting Review* 30, no. 4 (2021): 827–853.

15. Bourdieu, "La Fabrique des Débats Publics."

16. Pierre Bourdieu, *Sociology in Question* (London: Sage, 2003).

17. Richard J. Taffler, Crawford Spence, and Arman Eshraghi, "Emotional Economic Man: Calculation and Anxiety in Fund Management," *Accounting, Organizations and Society* 61 (2017): 53–67.

18. Marc Granovetter, "Economic Institutions as Social Constructions: A Framework for Analysis," *Acta Sociologica* 35 (1992): 3–11.

19. Hendrik Vollmer, Andrea Mennicken, and Alex Preda, "Tracking the Numbers: Across Accounting and Finance, Organizations and Markets," *Accounting, Organizations and Society* 34, no. 5 (2009): 619–637.

20. Peter Miller and Michael Power, "Accounting, Organizing, and Economizing: Connecting Accounting Research and Organization Theory," *Academy of Management Annals* 7, no. 1 (2013): 557–605.

5. TECHNOLOGICAL RESISTANCE

1. Andrew W. Lo, "What Is an Index?," *Journal of Portfolio Management* 42, no. 2 (2016): 21–36.

2. Robin Wigglesworth, *Trillions: How a Band of Wall Street Renegades Invented the Index Fund and Changed Finance Forever* (New York: Penguin, 2021), 18.

3. Donald MacKenzie, "Material Signals: A Historical Sociology of High-Frequency Trading," *American Journal of Sociology* 123, no. 6 (2018): 1635–1683.

4. Robert Seyfert, "Bugs, Predations or Manipulations? Incompatible Epistemic Regimes of High-Frequency Trading," *Economy and Society* 45, no. 2 (2016): 251–277.

5. Len Seabrooke, "Epistemic Arbitrage: Transnational Professional Knowledge in Action," *Journal of Professions and Organization* 1, no. 1 (2014): 49–64.

6. Pierre Bourdieu, *On the State* (Cambridge: Polity Press, 2014).

7. Richard J. Taffler, Crawford Spence, and Arman Eshraghi, "Emotional Economic Man: Calculation and Anxiety in Fund Management," *Accounting, Organizations and Society* 61 (2017): 53–67.

8. Greta Krippner, Mark Granovetter, Fred Block, Nicole Biggart, Tom Beamish, Youtien Hsing, Gillian Hart et al., "Polanyi Symposium: A Conversation on Embeddedness," *Socio-economic Review* 2, no. 1 (2004): 109–135.

9. Loïc Wacquant, "Symbolic Power and Group-Making: On Pierre Bourdieu's Reframing of Class," *Journal of Classical Sociology* 13, no. 2 (2013): 274–291.

10. Satish Kumar and Nisha Goyal, "Behavioural Biases in Investment Decision Making: A Systematic Literature Review," *Qualitative Research in Financial Markets* 7, no. 1 (2015): 88–108.

11. Daniel Susskind, *A World Without Work: Technology, Automation and How We Should Respond* (London: Penguin UK, 2020).

12. Gartner, "Information Technology Glossary," s.v. "Big Data," accessed July 8, 2024, https://www.gartner.com/en/information-technology/glossary/big-data.

13. Julapa Jagtiani and Catherine Lemieux, "The Roles of Alternative Data and Machine Learning in Fintech Lending: Evidence from the LendingClub Consumer Platform," *Financial Management* 48, no. 4 (2019): 1009–1029.

14. Leopold A. Bernstein, "In Defense of Fundamental Investment Analysis," *Financial Analysts Journal* 31, no. 1 (1975): 57–61.

15. Frank Pasquale, *The Black Box Society: The Secret Algorithms That Control Money and Information* (Cambridge, MA: Harvard University Press, 2015).

16. Pierre Bourdieu, *The Social Structures of the Economy* (Cambridge: Polity Press, 2005), 197.

17. Fabian Muniesa, Yuval Millo, and Michel Callon, "An Introduction to Market Devices," *Sociological Review* 55, no. 2 supp. (2007): 1–12.

18. Bingxu Fang, Ole Kristian Hope, Zhongwei Huang, and Rucsandra Moldovan, "The Effects of MiFID II on Sell-Side Analysts, Buy-Side Analysts, and Firms," *Review of Accounting Studies* 25 (2020): 855–902.

19. Generally underresearched as a group of actors, sales teams in investment banks work behind the sell-side analysts, promoting the latter's research

to buy-side clients, although an interesting study by Johan Graaf and Gustav Johed illustrates how significant conflicts can emerge between sales and research teams in investment banks when both compete for the attention of the buy-side. See Johan Graaf and Gustav Johed, "'Reverse Brokering' and the Consumption of Accounting: A Broker Desk Ethnography of an Investment Case," *Accounting, Organizations and Society* 85 (2020): art. 101154.

20. Howell E. Jackson and Jeffrey Zhang, "'Nobody Is Proud of Soft Dollars': The Impact of MiFID II on US Financial Markets," *Journal of Financial Regulation* 9, no. 2 (2023): 101–173.

21. Ludo Waltman, "A Review of the Literature on Citation Impact Indicators," *Journal of Informetrics* 10, no. 2 (2016): 365–391.

22. Crawford Spence, Mark Aleksanyan, Yuval Millo, Shahed Imam, and Subhash Abhayawansa, "Earning the 'Write to Speak': Sell-Side Analysts and Their Struggle to Be Heard," *Contemporary Accounting Research* 36, no. 4 (2019): 2635–2662.

23. Bourdieu, *On the State*, 184.

24. Bernstein, "In Defense of Fundamental Investment Analysis."

25. Seyfert, "Bugs, Predations or Manipulations?"

26. Seabrooke, "Epistemic Arbitrage."

6. THE BIG DOXIC DISTURBANCE

1. Emmanuel Levinas, *Alterity and Transcendence* (New York: Columbia University Press, 1999).

2. Pierre Bourdieu, *Outline of a Theory of Practice*, trans. Richard Nice (Cambridge: Cambridge University Press, 1977).

3. Leopold A. Bernstein, "In Defense of Fundamental Investment Analysis," *Financial Analysts Journal* 31, no. 1 (1975): 57–61.

4. Neil Fligstein and Doug McAdam, *A Theory of Fields* (New York: Oxford University Press, 2012).

5. Pierre Bourdieu, *Sociology in Question* (London: Sage, 2003), 73.

6. Pierre Bourdieu, *On the State* (Cambridge: Polity Press, 2014), 184.

7. Bingxu Fang, Ole Kristian Hope, Zhongwei Huang, and Rucsandra Moldovan, "The Effects of MiFID II on Sell-Side Analysts, Buy-Side Analysts, and Firms," *Review of Accounting Studies* 25 (2020): 855–902.

8. Alexander Ljungqvist, Felicia Marston, Laura T. Starks, Kelsey Wei, and Hong Yan, "Conflicts of Interest in Sell-Side Research and the

Moderating Role of Institutional Investors," *Journal of Financial Economics* 85, no. 2 (2007): 420–456.

9. See John Gittelsohn, "End of Era: Passive Equity Funds Surpass Active in Epic Shift," Bloomberg, September 11, 2019, https://www.bloomberg.com/news/articles/2019-09-11/passive-u-s-equity-funds-eclipse-active-in-epic-industry-shift; and Amy Whyte, "Active Managers Kept Losing Out to Passive, Even After Markets Crashed," Institutional Investor, January 25, 2021, https://www.institutionalinvestor.com/article/2bswmh848i74fdpofu134/portfolio/active-managers-kept-losing-out-to-passive-even-after-markets-crashed.

10. Eric Balchunas, *The Bogle Effect: How John Bogle and Vanguard Turned Wall Street Inside Out and Saved Investors Trillions* (Dallas: BenBella Books, 2022)

11. Morningstar, "Global Fund Flows 2024," https://www.morningstar.com/lp/global-asset-flows-report.

12. Investment Company Institute, *2023 Investment Company Fact Book* (Washington, DC: Investment Company Institute, 2023), https://www.ici.org/system/files/2023-05/2023-factbook.pdf.

13. Balchunas, *The Bogle Effect*, 125–126.

14. Steve Cohen is an American billionaire hedge fund manager.

15. Richard J. Taffler, Crawford Spence, and Arman Eshraghi, "Emotional Economic Man: Calculation and Anxiety in Fund Management," *Accounting, Organizations and Society* 61 (2017): 53–67.

16. Going "short" on a stock typically entails borrowing shares of said stock from a second-party financial intermediary for a fee. These borrowed shares are sold immediately to a third party and, once the price has gone down, bought back from the open market and then handed over to the second party, which loaned them in the first place. The hedge fund earns money by selling dear and buying cheap (minus the fee); the second party earns money from the fee it charges for loaning out fungible stock to the hedge fund; the third party may or may not lose depending on the price they bought the shares for in the first place.

17. Since conducting our interviews, the bull market has been disrupted by Covid-19, the war in Ukraine, and concomitant inflationary crises. Evidence suggests that passive investing has continued to outperform active investing during these periods. Laura Miller, "Less than 40% of Active Equity Managers Beat Average Passive Alternative in 2023," Investment Week, December 14, 2023, https://www.investmentweek.co.uk/news/4156437/active-equity-managers-beat-average-passive-fund-2023.

18. Balchunas, *The Bogle Effect*.
19. David A. Maber, Boris Groysberg, and Paul M. Healy, "An Empirical Examination of Sell-Side Brokerage Analysts' Published Research, Concierge Services, and High-Touch Services," *European Accounting Review* 30, no. 4 (2021): 827–853.
20. Dariusz Wójcik, "The Dark Side of NY–LON: Financial Centres and the Global Financial Crisis," *Urban Studies* 50, no. 13 (2013): 2736–2752.
21. Antonio Gramsci, Quention Hoare, and Geoffrey Nowell-Smith, *Selections from the Prison Notebooks of Antonio Gramsci* (New York: International Publishers, 1972).
22. Bourdieu, *Sociology in Question*.
23. Bourdieu, *On the State*.

7. DISTINCTION WORK

1. Leon Festinger, *A Theory of Cognitive Dissonance* (New York: Row, Peterson, 1957).
2. Scott James and Lucia Quaglia, "Epistemic Contestation and Interagency Conflict: The Challenge of Regulating Investment Funds," *Regulation and Governance* 17, no. 3 (2023): 346–362.
3. Davide Nicolini, Igor Pyrko, Omid Omidvar, and Agnessa Spanellis, "Understanding Communities of Practice: Taking Stock and Moving Forward," *Academy of Management Annals* 16, no. 2 (2022): 680–718.
4. S. G. Badrinath and Sunil Wahal, "Momentum Trading by Institutions," *Journal of Finance* 57, no. 6 (2002): 2449–2478.
5. Emmanuel Levinas, *Alterity and Transcendence* (New York: Columbia University Press, 1999).
6. Kenechukwu Anadu, Mathias Kruttli, Patrick McCabe, and Emilio Osambela, "The Shift from Active to Passive Investing: Risks to Financial Stability?," *Financial Analysts Journal* 76, no. 4 (2020): 23–39.
7. David Blitz, "The Dark Side of Passive Investing," *Journal of Portfolio Management* 41, no. 1 (2014): 1–4.
8. Ekkehart Boehmer and Juan Wu, "Short Selling and the Price Discovery Process," *Review of Financial Studies* 26, no. 2 (2013): 287–322.
9. Cristi A. Gleason and Charles M. Lee, "Analyst Forecast Revisions and Market Price Discovery," *Accounting Review* 78, no. 1 (2003): 193–225.
10. Shmuel Baruch and Xiaodi Zhang, "The Distortion in Prices due to Passive Investing," *Management Science* 68, no. 8 (2022): 6219–6234.

11. Eric Balchunas, *The Bogle Effect: How John Bogle and Vanguard Turned Wall Street Inside Out and Saved Investors Trillions* (Dallas: BenBella Books, 2022), 125–126.

12. Robin Wigglesworth, "Super Passive Goes Ballistic, Active Is Atrocious," *Financial Times*, January 19, 2023.

13. Emma Boyde, "Shift from Active to Passive Funds Is Accelerating, JP Morgan Says," *Financial Times*, November 23, 2022.

14. Balchunas, *The Bogle Effect*, 189–192.

15. Emile Van Duuren, Auke Plantinga, and Bert Scholtens, "ESG Integration and the Investment Management Process: Fundamental Investing Reinvented," *Journal of Business Ethics* 138 (2016): 525–533.

16. Max M. Schanzenbach and Robert H. Sitkoff, "Reconciling Fiduciary Duty and Social Conscience: The Law and Economics of ESG Investing by a Trustee," *Stanford Law Review* 72 (2020): 381–454.

17. Lauren Fedor and James Politi, "Joe Biden Expected to Issue First Presidential Veto in Anti-ESG Vote," *Financial Times*, March 1, 2023.

18. Crawford Spence, "Social Accounting's Emancipatory Potential: A Gramscian Critique," *Critical Perspectives on Accounting* 20, no. 2 (2009): 205–227.

19. Quoted in Kenneth P. Pucker and Andrew King, "ESG Investing Isn't Designed to Save the Planet," *Harvard Business Review*, August 1, 2022, https://hbr.org/2022/08/esg-investing-isnt-designed-to-save-the-planet.

20. Marco D'Eramo, "Jet-Setters," *Sidecar* (blog), March 10, 2023, https://newleftreview.org/sidecar/posts/jet-setters.

21. Spence, "Social Accounting's Emancipatory Potential."

22. Daniel Giamouridis, "Systematic Investment Strategies," *Financial Analysts Journal* 73, no. 4 (2017): 10–14.

23. Balchunas, *The Bogle Effect*.

24. Nicolini et al., "Understanding Communities of Practice."

25. In addition to the studies already cited, see Lubos Pástor and M. Blair Vorsatz, "Mutual Fund Performance and Flows During the COVID-19 Crisis," *Review of Asset Pricing Studies* 10, no. 4 (2020): 791–833; and Ben Johnson, "Morningstar's Active/Passive Barometer," Morningstar, June 16, 2021, https://www.morningstar.com/lp/active-passive-barometer.

26. Nicolini et al., "Understanding Communities of Practice."

27. Two excellent articles by Adam Hayes illustrate this point very clearly: "Enacting a Rational Actor: Roboadvisors and the Algorithmic Performance of Ideal Types," *Economy and Society* 49, no. 4 (2020): 562–595; and

"The Active Construction of Passive Investors: Roboadvisors and Algorithmic 'Low-Finance,'" *Socio-economic Review* 19, no. 1 (2021): 83–110.

28. Robert Seyfert, "Bugs, Predations or Manipulations? Incompatible Epistemic Regimes of High-Frequency Trading," *Economy and Society* 45, no. 2 (2016): 251–277.

CONCLUSION: PURPOSEFUL INERTIA IN FINANCIAL MARKETS

1. David Hirshleifer, "Presidential Address: Social Transmission Bias in Economics and Finance," *Journal of Finance* 75, no. 4 (2020): 1779–1831.

2. David Hirshleifer, "Behavioral Finance," *Annual Review of Economics* 7 (2015): 133–159.

3. Marc Granovetter, "Economic Institutions as Social Constructions: A Framework for Analysis," *Acta Sociologica* 35 (1992): 3–11.

4. Pierre Bourdieu, *The Social Structures of the Economy* (Cambridge: Polity Press, 2005).

5. Scott James and Lucia Quaglia, "Epistemic Contestation and Interagency Conflict: The Challenge of Regulating Investment Funds," *Regulation and Governance* 17, no. 3 (2023): 346–362.

6. Karl Marx, *Capital: A Critique of Political Economy, Volume I*, trans. Ben Fowkes (London: Penguin, 1992).

7. Pierre Bourdieu, *Sociology in Question* (London: Sage, 2003).

8. Lauren A. Rivera, "Hiring as Cultural Matching: The Case of Elite Professional Service Firms," *American Sociological Review* 77, no. 6 (2012): 999–1022.

9. Chris Carter and Crawford Spence, "Being a Successful Professional: An Exploration of Who Makes Partner in the Big Four," *Contemporary Accounting Research* 31, no. 4 (2014): 949–981.

10. Bourdieu, *Sociology in Question*, 73.

11. Neil Fligstein and Doug McAdam, *A Theory of Fields* (New York: Oxford University Press, 2012).

12. Pierre Bourdieu, *Outline of a Theory of Practice*, trans. Richard Nice (Cambridge: Cambridge University Press, 1977).

13. Max Weber, *The Sociology of Religion* (Boston: Beacon Press, 1993). We first came across this quote in "Jet-Setters," written by Marco D'Eramo for the *New Left Review*'s *Sidecar* blog, March 10, 2023, https://newleftreview.org/sidecar/posts/jet-setters.

14. C. Wright Mills, *The Power Elite* (Oxford: Oxford University Press, 1956).

15. Benjamin Braun, "Asset Manager Capitalism as a Corporate Governance Regime," in *The American Political Economy: Politics, Markets, and Power*, ed. Jacob S. Hacker, Alexander Hertel-Fernandez, Paul Pierson, and Kathleen Thelen (Cambridge: Cambridge University Press, 2021), 270–294.

16. Hirshleifer, "Behavioral Finance."

17. See, for example, Fabian Muniesa, Yuval Millo, and Michel Callon, "An Introduction to Market Devices," *Sociological Review* 55, no. 2 supp. (2007): 1–12; Donald MacKenzie, "Material Signals: A Historical Sociology of High-Frequency Trading," *American Journal of Sociology* 123, no. 6 (2018): 1635–1683; and Juan-Pablo Pardo-Guerra, *Automating Finance: Infrastructures, Engineers, and the Making of Electronic Markets* (Cambridge: Cambridge University Press, 2019).

18. Paul A. David, "Clio and the Economics of QWERTY," *American Economic Review* 75, no. 2 (1985): 332–337.

19. Steven Suranovic, "Fossil Fuel Addiction and the Implications for Climate Change Policy," *Global Environmental Change* 23, no. 3 (2013): 598–608.

20. Leon Festinger, *A Theory of Cognitive Dissonance* (New York: Row, Peterson, 1957).

21. Eric Balchunas, *The Bogle Effect: How John Bogle and Vanguard Turned Wall Street Inside Out and Saved Investors Trillions* (Dallas: BenBella Books, 2022).

22. Diane-Laure Arjaliès, Philip Grant, Iain Hardie, Donald A. MacKenzie, and Ekaterina Svetlova, *Chains of Finance: How Investment Management Is Shaped* (Oxford: Oxford University Press, 2017).

23. Braun, "Asset Manager Capitalism."

24. Balchunas, *The Bogle Effect*, 235.

25. Adam S. Hayes, "The Active Construction of Passive Investors: Roboadvisors and Algorithmic 'Low-Finance,'" *Socio-economic Review* 19, no. 1 (2021): 83–110.

26. Robin Blackburn, "Finance and the Fourth Dimension," *New Left Review* 39 (May/June 2006).

27. Arjaliès et al., *Chains of Finance*.

28. Although on wealth managers, see Brooke Harrington, *Capital Without Borders: Wealth Managers and the One Percent* (Cambridge, MA: Harvard University Press, 2016).

29. Lubos Pástor and M. Blair Vorsatz, "Mutual Fund Performance and Flows During the COVID-19 Crisis," *Review of Asset Pricing Studies* 10, no. 4 (2020): 791–833.

30. Balchunas, *The Bogle Effect*; Robin Wigglesworth, *Trillions: How a Band of Wall Street Renegades Invented the Index Fund and Changed Finance Forever* (New York: Penguin, 2021).

31. CRED, "Beware of the Index Huggers," January 21, 2022, https://cred.club /articles/beware-of-the-index-huggers.

METHODOLOGICAL APPENDIX:
SPEAKING TO THE PROPHETS OF ALPHA

1. Alan Bryman, "The Debate About Quantitative and Qualitative Research: A Question of Method or Epistemology?," *British Journal of Sociology* 35, no. 1 (1984): 75–92.

2. Mario Luis Small, "'How Many Cases Do I Need?' On Science and the Logic of Case Selection in Field-Based Research," *Ethnography* 10, no. 1 (2009): 5–38.

3. Mark N. K. Saunders and Keith Townsend, "Reporting and Justifying the Number of Interview Participants in Organization and Workplace Research," *British Journal of Management* 27, no. 4 (2016): 836–852.

4. Glenn A. Bowen, "Naturalistic Inquiry and the Saturation Concept: A Research Note," *Qualitative Research* 8, no. 1 (2008): 137–152.

5. Laura Miller, "Investment Team Hiring Still 2:1 Male Dominated," Investment Week, November 1, 2022, https://www.investmentweek.co.uk /news/4059321/investment-team-hiring-male-dominated.

6. For this, we largely followed what has come to be known as the Gioia method, following the work on this by Denis Gioia. See, for example, Shawn M. Clark, Denis A. Gioia, David J. Ketchen, and James Thomas, "Transitional Identity as a Facilitator of Organizational Identity Change During a Merger," *Administrative Science Quarterly* 55 (2010): 397; and Denis A. Gioia, Kevin Corley, and Aimee L. Hamilton, "Seeking Qualitative Rigor in Inductive Research: Notes on the Gioia Methodology," *Organizational Research Methods* 16, no. 1 (2013): 15–31.

7. Michele Lamont, "How Has Bourdieu Been Good to Think With? The Case of the United States," *Sociological Forum* 27, no. 1 (2012): 228–237.

8. Thomas Ahrens and Chris Chapman, "Doing Qualitative Field Research in Management Accounting: Positioning Data to Contribute to Theory," *Accounting, Organizations and Society* 31, no. 8 (2006): 819–841.

9. Neil Fligstein and Doug McAdam, *A Theory of Fields* (New York: Oxford University Press, 2012), 168.

10. Pierre Bourdieu, *Practical Reason* (Cambridge: Polity Press, 1998), 76.

11. Nick Crossley, *Towards Relational Sociology* (London: Routledge, 2011).

12. Moin Syed and Sarah C. Nelson, "Guidelines for Establishing Reliability When Coding Narrative Data," *Emerging Adulthood* 3, no. 6 (2015): 375–387.

13. John Campbell, Charles Quincy, Jordan Osserman, and Ove K. Pedersen, "Coding In-Depth Semistructured Interviews: Problems of Unitization and Intercoder Reliability and Agreement," *Sociological Methods & Research* 42, no. 3 (2013): 294–320.

14. Loïc Wacquant, "Towards a Reflexive Sociology: A Workshop with Pierre Bourdieu," *Sociological Theory* 7, no. 1 (1989): 26–63.

15. See also Pierre Bourdieu and Loïc Wacquant, *An Invitation to Reflexive Sociology* (Cambridge: Polity Press, 1992).

16. Stefan Leins, *Stories of Capitalism* (Chicago: University of Chicago Press, 2018).

INDEX

accurate forecasting: analysts, 27–28; higher value, 28; lower value, 27

action: economic, 4, 9–10, 39–40, 42–43, 46–47, 106, 179, 186; social, 182

active fund management community, 7, 104, 178, 180, 188, 195, 202

active fund managers, 18, 141, 148; and benchmarks, 170–171; and doxic disturbance, 152–153; and low-cost index funds, 2

active funds, 4, 18, 23; defensiveness, 170; organizational cultures, 117; and passive investment/funds, 139, 146, 161

active investing, 4, 8, 136, 139, 141–143, 152, 155–156

active investment community, 2, 4, 7, 52, 105–109, 122–123, 109, 160; cognitive structures of, 127;

epistemic regime of, 135–136, 141, 146–147

active investment game, 204

actor-network theory (ANT), 47–48, 186–187

ADViCE framework, 29

agonistic logic, 49, 97

algorithmically oriented funds, 159

alpha generation, 93, 100, 105, 107–108, 142, 168, 170, 173

ambivalence, 64, 132, 183

American Finance Association, 38

analysts: accurate forecasting, 27–28; acquire buy-side votes, 30–32; and asset managers, 31; buy-side, 13, 19–24; and consensus numbers, 83–84; generate informed insights, 26–27; make accurate stock recommendations, 28–29; motivate others to act,

analysts (*continued*)
  29–30; sell-side, 13, 19–24;
  spending time, 25–32. *See also*
  buy-side investment firms/
  analysts; sell-side investment
  firms/analysts
AnalystSolutions, 26
Arjaliès, Diane-Laure, 13, 17, 20–21, 185
artificial intelligence, 109–123; buy-
  side views, 109–119; sell-side
  views, 119–123
asset allocators, 209n1
asset manager capitalism, 184, 189
asset managers: active, 18; and
  analysts, 31; asset manager
  capitalism, 184, 189; investment
  decision-making, 3
assets under management (AUM),
  173, 189

Balchunas, Eric, 141, 171
bear markets, 144, 167–171
behavioral finance, 36–39, 59,
  106, 179
Biden, Joe, 172
big data, 109–123; buy-side views,
  109–119; sell-side views, 119–123
Blackrock, 176, 189
Bloomberg, 83, 85, 172, 186
BlueMatrix, 128–129
Bogle, Jack, 141
boldness in financial markets, 10,
  84, 101
Bourdieu, Pierre, 4, 7, 40–43, 47, 51,
  55, 185
brokerage capacity, 73

broker stickiness: bundling, 70–77;
  internal divisions on buy-side,
  77–80
Brown, Lawrence, 31
bull market, 143–144, 167–169, 176,
  220n17
bundling, 70–77
buy-side investment firms/analysts,
  13, 19–24; interorganizational
  dependencies, 71–73;
  interpersonal ties with sell-
  side firms, 59–66; on sell-side
  analysts' forecasts, 76; on sell-side
  quality of research, 72–74, 76
buy-side views: artificial intelligence,
  109–119; big data, 109–119;
  machine learning, 109–119

Callon, Michel, 46–47
capital: cultural, 40; defined, 49;
  economic, 2, 46; endowments of,
  97; social, 42, 46; symbolic, 46
capitalism: asset manager, 184, 189;
  organic intellectuals, 151
Chartered Financial Analysts
  Society (CFAS), 24, 31
Christophers, Brett, 209n2
CNBC, 192
coder reliability, 204
Cohen, Steve, 142, 220n14
communities of practice, 155, 185,
  192
communities under threat, 5, 11,
  155–156
company management, 26, 31, 65–71,
  81, 84, 139

concomitant inflationary crises, 220n17
conduit for volume, 75
congealed social relations, 2, 105–106, 133, 178, 185, 191–192
consensus numbers: and analysts, 83–84; as centripetal force, 85–88, 92–101; criticisms of, 97–101; divergence from, 93–97; and fund managers, 90; as safe, 89–92
corporate behavior, 175
corporate finance, 22, 71–72, 76
corporate governance, 35, 189
Covid-19 pandemic, 169–170, 203, 220n17
Craftsman, The (Sennett), 6
Cramer, Jim, 192
cultural matching, 63
cultural norms, 40–41, 181
customer relationship management systems, 123–127

data coding, 205
"defensive discourse of orthodoxy," 183
differentiated opinion, 93, 95, 102
distinction work, 154–178; bear markets, 167–171; communities under threat, 155–156; ethical investing, 171–176; price discovery, 161–167; price distortions, 156–161
distinctiveness, 93, 97, 101
doxa, 55; defined, 135; epistemic, 49
doxic anxiety, 135

doxic disturbance, 134–153; passive investing, 145–152; shrinking ecosystem, 136–145
Durkheim, Emile, 55

EBITDA, 68, 215n13
economic action, 4, 9–10, 39–40, 42–43, 46–47, 106, 179, 186
economic behavior: oversocialized view of, 43; undersocialized view of, 42–43
economic relations, 181
ecosystem: corporate/industry, 65; shrinking, 136–145
efficient market hypothesis (EMH), 49–50
engrained mental schemata, 106
environmental, social, and governance (ESG) investing, 171–175, 189
epistemic arbiters/gatekeepers, 133
epistemic contestation, 50, 154
epistemic doxa, 49
epistemic regime, 5, 105; of active investment community, 135–136, 141, 146–147; financial intermediaries, 49
epistemic schisms, 49–52
epistemological chauvinism, 155
ethical investing, 171–176
Europe: and ESG, 171; large-cap pharmaceuticals stocks, 202; MiFID II regulation in, 72, 124, 126
exchange-traded funds (ETFs), 135, 159–161, 192. See also index funds

exchange-traded fund (ETF) SPY, 2, 16, 135, 159, 192
expert networks, 11, 16, 64–65, 81

field: defined, 45; dynamics, 46; and inertia, 58; norms in, 66–70; position, 10, 52, 82, 84, 105, 151, 178, 181, 183–187, 189; social, 45–48; social dynamics of, 84; social structure of, 62, 64
financial forecasts, 27–29, 60, 80
financial intermediaries, 1–2, 5–7, 34, 186; academic literature on, 33; criticism of, 36; epistemic regimes, 49; and investment chain, 13–19; orthodox literature on, 34
financial intermediation, 1–3, 9, 11, 13–14, 17–19, 36, 56, 192
financial markets, 1–4, 9–12; dominant frames of, 33–36; future research directions, 190–193; purposeful inertia in, 179–193; rethinking, 185–187; social structures of, 33–53
financial markets 4.0, 106–108
Fligstein, Neil, 51–52, 185
fossil-fuel addiction, 188
fundamental analysis, 133
fund management communities, 202. See also active fund management community
funds: algorithmically oriented, 159; exchange-traded, 135, 159–161, 192; hedge, 14, 16, 76, 112–113,

167, 220n16; index, 135, 148–150; quantitative, 111, 116. See also active funds; passive funds

Galbraith, John Kenneth, 1–2
GAMMA PI model, 26
Gerson Lehrman Group, 64
Gioia, Denis, 225n6
Gioia method, 225n6
going "short" on a stock, 220n16
Google Scholar, 129
Graaf, Johan, 218–219n19
Granovetter, Marc, 4, 42–44, 47, 185

habit, and financial markets analysis, 55
habitus, 45, 59; hypothesis-driven, 133, 136, 156, 193
hanging out, 61
Hayes, Adam, 222n27
hedge funds, 14, 16, 76, 112–113, 167, 220n16
herding in financial markets, 10
heuristics, 37
high-frequency traders, 105
Hirshleifer, David, 37–40, 179
human cognition and intuition, 117, 120
human empathy, 182
hypothesis-driven habitus, 133, 136, 156, 193

illusio, 55–56, 95, 97, 102, 146
index fund pioneers, 192
index funds, 135, 148–150. See also exchange-traded funds (ETFs)

index investing, 104, 189; growth of, 177, 180; oligopolistic nature of, 189; price distortive effects of, 156

industry competency model, 25–26

inertia: and field, 58; and investment advice, 59; purposeful, 180–185

information intermediaries, 34

informed insights: analysts, 26–27; higher value, 27; lower value, 26–27

innovative/software-mediated processing, 109

institutional clients, 2

interpersonal ties, 59–70

"interpretive community," 204

investing: active, 4, 8, 136, 139, 141–143, 152, 155–156; ethical, 171–176; future of, 188–190; index (*See* index investing); passive, 145–152, 184–185

investment banks/banking activity, 22; bulge-bracket, 202; business model of, 121; buy-side firms, 23; sell-side analysts from, 3, 16, 72, 77; structure, 21–22

investment chain: and financial intermediaries, 13–19; high-profile criticisms of, 18; levels of, 14–16, 20–21

Investment Company Institute, 18, 141

Investopedia, 1

James, Scott, 50

Johed, Gustav, 218–219n19

Kahneman, Daniel, 36

La Distinction (Bourdieu), 40

Latour, Bruno, 46

Levinas, Emmanuel, 158

London Stock Exchange, 16

long-only mutual funds, 16

long/short hedge funds, 16

Luddism, 108, 134

machine learning, 109–123; buy-side views, 109–119; sell-side views, 119–123

Mad Money, 192

Marx, Karl, 40

material infrastructures, 186

material power, 105, 151

McAdam, Doug, 51–52, 185

microseconds, 104

MiFID II regulations, 72, 124, 126

modern portfolio theory, 177

Morningstar, 18, 85, 141

New York Stock Exchange, 16

Nicolini, Davide, 185

nonhuman objects, 186

note-tracking software, 128–132

NVivo qualitative data software, 203

obligatory passage point, 89, 102

organizational cultures, 117

orthodoxy, 135, 151

Our Lives in Their Portfolios: Why Asset Managers Own the World (Christophers), 209n1

oversocialized view of economic behavior, 43, 64

passive community, 155–156, 161, 168–169, 172, 177, 180, 184, 188, 191, 193

passive fund managers, 141

passive funds, 8, 18, 32, 143–147, 175; distortive effects of, 161; economic downturn, 168; and free float, 161

passive investing, 145–152, 184–185

passive investment community, 4, 52, 133, 135, 158, 191–192

price discovery, 161–167

price distortions, 156–161

price targets, 5, 60, 80, 195

Property, Plant & Equipment (PP&E), 142–143

Protestant Ethic and the Spirit of Capitalism, The (Weber), 40

purposeful inertia, 8–9, 178, 180–185

Python, 116

Quaglia, Lucia, 50

quantitative funds, 111, 116

QWERTY keyboard, 188

rationality-related approaches, 59

relational sociology, 204

religious cults, 188

research note consumption, 131

Russian dolls approach, 52

Scopus, 129

secondary market, 16

second-party financial intermediary, 220n16

self-styled investment elite, and consensus, 93

sell-side investment firms/analysts, 13, 19–24; commissions, 72–73; conduit for volume, 75; and field norms, 66–70; generation of corporate finance work, 71; interpersonal ties with buy-side firms, 59–66; and investment banks, 71–72, 77; quality of research, 72–74, 76. *See also* analysts

sell-side views: artificial intelligence, 119–123; big data, 119–123; machine learning, 119–123

Sennett, Richard, 6

shrinking ecosystem, 136–145

smart beta, 193

social action, 182

social capital, 42, 46, 181

social environment, 204

social fields, 45–48

social finance, 36–39, 179

social networks, 42–45

social relations: congealed, 2, 105–106, 133, 178, 185, 191–192; and economics, 40

social stickiness, 5, 54–82; broker stickiness, 70–77; habit, 55–59; long-term interpersonal ties, 59–70

social structures, 40–42; of financial markets, 33–53

Social Structures of the Economy, The (Bourdieu), 40

social transmission bias, 39

S&P 500, 148, 157, 189
stock ratings, 60
stock recommendations: analysts,
    28–29; higher value, 28–29; lower
    value, 28
synergistic EBITDA, 68

technological innovation, 2,
    128, 132
technological resistance, 104–133;
    artificial intelligence, 109–123;
    big data, 109–123; clocking
    up the billable hours, 123–132;
    financial markets 4.0, 106–
    108; machine learning,
    109–123

threat: communities under, 5, 11,
    155–156; existential, 156, 175,
    180–181; exogenous, 151
tiered structure, 80
Tversky, Amos, 36

Ukraine war, 220n17
undersocialized view of economic
    behavior, 42–43
U.S. Labor Department, 172

Vanguard, 141, 176, 189
Visible Alpha, 85

Wall Street, 95
Weber, Max, 40, 55, 184

GPSR Authorized Representative: Easy Access System Europe, Mustamäe tee 50, 10621 Tallinn, Estonia, gpsr.requests@easproject.com

www.ingramcontent.com/pod-product-compliance
Lightning Source LLC
Chambersburg PA
CBHW032130020426
42334CB00016B/1102